A PRACTICAL GUIDE TO STAMP DUTY LAND TAX

Mark Stapleton, David Gubbay,
Sam Moore and Eli Hillman of Dechert LLP

LEGALEASE
PUBLISHING

ISBN: 1-903927-40-4

Published by Legalease Publishing, Kensington Square House, 12-14 Ansdell Street, London W8 5BN

Printed and bound in Great Britain by Martins, Berwick upon Tweed

www.legalease.co.uk

Contents

Contents

FOREWORD

Stamp duty land tax (SDLT) represents yet another major change in the tax rules relevant to transactions in UK-situate property. Unlike stamp duty, which for over 300 years has been a tax on documents, SDLT is a transaction-based tax. SDLT is also a modern tax in terms of its approach to self-assessment and compliance. This will be a source of great discomfort for taxpayers and advisers alike, and this book has been written with this in mind.

The book is intended to be, first and foremost, a practical guide to SDLT rather than a detailed technical guide. My co-authors and I have tried to focus on the key questions and issues that will face taxpayers and advisers in relation to common UK property transactions. We have also tried to include the key reference materials for SDLT in the CD-Rom that comes with this book.

We have timed the release of this publication so that the book takes into account both the primary legislation in the Finance Act 2003 and also the regulations issued subsequently. We have also seen the current guidance provided by the Inland Revenue in its Manual. However, although the Inland Revenue has sought to provide helpful guidance on a range of issues, including informal guidance given on certain issues referred to in this book. Because SDLT is a new tax, there is considerable uncertainty and scope for differing views on many aspects of the tax. There will inevitably be a stream of further guidance issued and developing jurisprudence as the tax beds down and this will of course impact upon the views expressed in this book. This book represents the views and understanding of the authors as at 1 March 2004.

Whilst much of the guidance provided is relevant to residential transactions, our main focus has been on the application of SDLT to commercial property transactions. The material is based upon prevailing UK law and issues of particular relevance to Scotland or Northern Ireland have not been addressed, save where specifically stated in the text.

In addition to my co-authors and, in particular, Eli Hillman who has borne much of the brunt of the initial drafting and editing of the material, I am grateful to Emma Slessenger for her indispensable comments from a property practitioner's perspective and her experienced editorial input, without which this book would not have been possible.

I am also grateful for the support of Legalease to this publication and for their understanding and flexibility in relation to deadlines.

Mark Stapleton,
March 2004

ABOUT THE AUTHORS

Mark Stapleton is a partner and is head of the tax unit at Dechert. He advises on UK and international direct and indirect taxation issues. This includes property acquisitions, development projects, securitisations, structured finance and a variety of other banking, financial and corporate transactions. He is a past national secretary of the VAT Practitioners Group and an associate of the Chartered Institute of Taxation. He is also a member of the taxation committee of the British Retail Consortium and the International Fiscal Association. He is a regular speaker at conferences, particularly those focusing on the property sector. He graduated from Nottingham University with an LL.B in 1985 and joined Dechert in 1993, becoming a partner in 1996.

David Gubbay is a partner in the Dechert tax unit. He has considerable experience in all areas of direct and indirect tax, and advises on a wide variety of property, corporate, investment fund and finance matters. In the property arena, he advises on property development and investment matters, joint venture structures and property funds. He is a regular speaker at conferences on tax issues, in particular on property tax matters. He is graduate of Rhodes University and of Magdalen College, Oxford. He joined Dechert in 1999 and became a partner in 2001.

Sam Moore is a solicitor who advises on UK and international direct and indirect tax issues, including mergers and acquisitions, reorganisations, property acquisitions and cross-border transactions. Prior to joining Dechert he worked for another major City law firm for three and a half years. He is a graduate of the University of Adelaide (Bachelor of Economics, 1992 and Bachelor of Laws (with Hons), 1995 and the University of New South Wales (Master in Taxation, 1998). He was admitted to practice in South Australia in October 1996 and in England in March 2002.

Eli Hillman is a solicitor in the Dechert tax unit. He advises on all aspects of direct and indirect taxation, including in relation to mergers & acquisitions, investment funds, property transactions and cross-border matters. Eli spent the period from February to September 2003 (representing much of the SDLT consultation period) seconded to the British Property Federation, putting forward the industry position on SDLT and other property taxation matters. He graduated with a an LL.B from Kings College London in 1995, and a masters degree in law from Mansfield College, Oxford in 1996 before qualifying as a solicitor at Dechert in October 2000.

CD-ROM

The full texts of selected statutory and other materials referred to in this book can be found on the CD-Rom attached to the inside back cover:

Statutes and statutory instruments:

- Finance Act 2003, Part 4 and Schedules 3-19 (consolidated following SI 2003/2816)
- The Stamp Duty (Disadvantaged Areas) Regulations 2001
- The Stamp Duty Land Tax (Administration) Regulations 2003
- The Stamp Duty Land Tax (Consequential Amendment of Enactments) Regulations 2003
- The Stamp Duty and Stamp Duty Land Tax (Consequential Amendment of Enactments) Regulations 2003
- The Stamp Duty Land Tax (Appointment of the Implementation Date) Order 2003
- The Stamp Duty Land Tax (Amendment of Schedule 4 to the Finance Act 2003) Regulations 2003

Inland Revenue materials:

- Inland Revenue return forms SDLT1, SDLT2, SDLT3, SDLT4 and SDLT60.
- Stamp Duty Land Tax Manual
- Enquiries under Stamp Duty Land Tax
- SP1/2003: Stamp Duty: Disadvantaged Areas Relief
- Customer Newsletters 1-4
- Stamp Duty Information Bulletin, Issue 6

Other materials:

- Stamp Duty Land Tax on Lease Transactions Calculator
- Stamp Office Addresses, Telephone Numbers and Opening Hours

Table of Cases

TABLE OF STATUTES

1. Introduction and overview

Why is SDLT important?

1.01 All those concerned with the ownership, development, financing or management of property will be affected by the introduction of stamp duty land tax (SDLT) because of its direct impact on the pricing of transactions and the potentially extensive exposure to interest and penalties introduced by the new rules. Conveyancing lawyers in particular will have to give more advice, particularly on the compliance requirements arising from the introduction of SDLT.

1.02 SDLT has been portrayed by the Inland Revenue as a modernisation of stamp duty. The reality is that it is a completely new transaction-based tax which has nothing whatsoever to do with the stamping of documents. The scope of SDLT is significantly wider than stamp duty and, whilst the headline rates of duty have not been increased, the amount of tax raised is likely to rise significantly because of the more limited scope for avoidance and the basis upon which the consideration is calculated. In particular, non-monetary consideration will, much like value added tax (VAT), be taken into account, as will all rents payable under a lease rather than an annual average rental, in applying the relevant rate of charge. In addition, compliance obligations are greatly increased under the SDLT regime and, much like other self-assessed taxes, unpaid tax will become assessable as a debt due to the Crown. In particular, unlike stamp duty, deliberate non-payment of SDLT, when it is known by the taxpayer to be properly, due will constitute a criminal offence.

1.03 Certain aspects of the tax, such as the charge on rents payable under a lease, the treatment of transactions such as sale and leasebacks, PFI transactions and certain compliance matters have been amended in Regulations issued since the enactment of the Finance Act 2003, following consultation carried out with property industry representative groups and other interested parties. Those changes are reflected in this book.

Why was SDLT introduced?

1.04 In April 2002, the government announced a consultation exercise to reform stamp duty on land and buildings. The rationale for change was said to be based on three key issues – modernisation, e-business/conveyancing and fairness. No one could really deny that stamp duty needed modernisation – after all, it had been around in substantially the same form for over 300 years. Certainly, the concept of impressing stamps on documents is antiquated. However, equally it would have been possible to modify and codify stamp duty without abandoning much of the existing legislation. There is also the desire to bring the legislation into line with electronic conveyancing, although it is unlikely that this will be implemented, in terms of instantaneous online registration of transactions, until at least 2007, so the rush to push through SDLT by December 2003 cannot be justified on this basis. Furthermore, SDLT is not yet compatible with instantaneous online registration, as in most cases it requires the taxpayer to complete an extensive land transaction return and obtain certification from the Inland Revenue following a transaction before registration is permitted. Indeed, it is likely that the registration process will be slower in many cases.

1.05 This leaves the residual concept of 'fairness', which of course begs the question of fairness to whom? In short, the Treasury's answer to this is that a 4% rate of duty to be paid by all on transactions in excess of £500,000 and a substantial increase in the duty payable on leases is fair.

1.06 As referred to in **para 1.05** above, in relation to leases, SDLT brings with it a much-increased basis of tax. A system based on charging tax at 1% on the net present value (NPV) of rents payable throughout the term of the lease was hastily announced in the 2003 Budget, subject to the possibility of altering the regime in response to a consultation then announced by the Chancellor of the Exchequer, Gordon Brown. The basis announced would have increased lease duty in many cases by between four and eight times the level paid on each lease under stamp duty. In the Chancellor's speech, there was an indication[1] that tax avoidance was sometimes the motivation for choosing to take a lease rather than a freehold interest and that leases needed to be taxed on an increased basis to prevent this. Industry representatives raised the objection that the choice of a lease is based on commercial considerations, and that a lease is in no way interchangeable with a freehold. Furthermore, it was argued on their behalf that rack rental occupational leases (representing the vast majority of commercial leases) have little or no value in accounting terms, and thus should not be subject to tax in the tenant's hands. While there was some recognition by the Inland Revenue that leases are not used for avoidance purposes, and in a string of meetings the Inland Revenue considered various alternative regimes suggested by industry, ultimately none of these suggestions was accepted. A minor concession only was made to apply the exempt bands on a 'slice' rather than 'slab' basis, such that leases with an NPV in excess of the exempt threshold would pay SDLT only in relation to the proportion of the NPV that exceeds the threshold. Undoubtedly, Treasury concerns regarding the state of the public purse were behind the limited concession given, but the result has been disappointing to industry representatives, who justifiably insist that leases should not be seen as a soft target for stamp taxation. The small concession made does not greatly assist the position of large commercial leases, for which tax will still have increased by four to eight or more times the tax levied under the old stamp duty regime.

---

1 Budget 2003 speech, transcript, p 16.

1.07 At the heart of the drive for change is the Treasury's desire to raise further tax, both by extending the scope of stamp duty, and by closing loopholes which had been exploited extensively in recent years, particularly in the context of high-value commercial property transactions. Whether SDLT proves to be successful in this respect remains to be seen. Tax planners have the ability to use techniques involving partnerships until the draft legislation relating to partnerships is implemented, probably in the Finance Act 2004. By then, further ideas will have emerged to supplement those that already exist. Importantly, however, the stakes will have become higher for those engaging in avoidance because of the new extensive self-assessment compliance regime under SDLT, which was not a feature of stamp duty. Although the land transaction return does not contain a box for 'other information', taxpayers who seek to mitigate tax will need to make sure that it is evident from the information provided that they have adequately disclosed the details of the transaction on the return or by letter to the Inland Revenue (or a Stamp Office) in order to limit the time period for potential challenge as far as possible.

1.08 Despite the constant battle against avoidance, stamp duty has proved to be a tax of increasing importance to the Inland Revenue and is relatively straightforward to collect. According to Inland Revenue figures, whereas in the 1997-98 tax year capital gains tax, inheritance tax and stamp duty on land and property all raised approximately the same amount of revenue (£1,400m-£1,700m) provisional figures for the 2002-2003 tax year suggest that stamp duty will significantly outstrip the aggregate amounts raised from both capital taxes, producing an anticipated £5,000m of revenue. SDLT will require greater Inland Revenue manpower to police the ongoing audit process but, at the same time, the need to impress stamps on documents is removed. The latter is of benefit to the taxpayer as it should prevent the need to automatically submit original property documents (which have been known to go astray) to the Inland Revenue.

From when is SDLT relevant?

1.09 SDLT has replaced stamp duty in relation to virtually all property transactions with effect from 1 December 2003.[2] More specifically, SDLT will apply to transactions completed after that date except where a contract relating to the transaction has been entered into on or before 10 July 2003. However, if such a contract has been varied or amended in some way after 10 July 2003 a transaction completed after 1 December 2003 will be within the scope of SDLT. Further, where an option or right of pre-emption is acquired before 1 December 2003 but on or after 17 April 2003, any consideration given for that option or right of pre-emption will be taken into account for SDLT purposes where, broadly speaking, the option or right of pre-emption is exercised on or after 1 December 2003. A similar provision applies in relation to variations of options on or after 17 April 2003.

What are the implications of SDLT for property advisers?

1.10 Property advisers will need to familiarise themselves with the new rules relevant to SDLT. New opportunities for mitigation will need to be explored at an early stage when possible transactions are being discussed. Furthermore, the taxpayer should consider how best to organise the ownership of its property interests in order to permit planning to be facilitated, should a transaction take place at a future date. Having implemented a transaction, conveyancers will need to give careful consideration to the completion of the land transaction return (even in terms of the right colour ink to use!) and whether adequate disclosure of a transaction is made in the return. There is now also the possibility of further returns being required in the light

---

2 Finance Act 2003, Sch 19 and Stamp Duty Land Tax (Appointment of the Implementation Date) Order 2003, reg 1. Throughout this book, references to primary legislation are to the Finance Act 2003 unless otherwise stated.

of circumstances arising after the transaction date. If the conveyancer is not to be responsible for determining and completing further returns, the taxpayer needs to be notified of this possibility so that responsibility is properly allocated to avoid exposure to additional tax penalties and interest upon audit. The Law Society has also provided guidance on practice issues which practitioners should consider.[3]

1.11 The Inland Revenue is currently gearing up for the audit process. Taxpayers will be for the most part selected for audit on a risk-assessed basis and it is expected that the net will be cast widely during the early years of the tax. Given this, taxpayers and their advisers must ensure that records are kept so that the audit process can be satisfied in a way which keeps tax, penalties and professional costs to a minimum. The Inland Revenue has promised to adopt a 'light touch' with taxpayers in the first few months of SDLT, but this should not lead to complacency on the part of taxpayers and their advisers.[4]

Remnants of stamp duty

1.12 Stamp duty is not yet dead and buried. It will continue to apply to transactions in shares and marketable securities and certain bearer instruments. In addition, it also will have potential application in relation to certain property transactions involving partnerships, such as the sale of interests in partnerships and certain transfers of property into or out of partnerships. These transactions are expressly exempted from SDLT,[5] although draft clauses have been issued with a view to bringing them within the scope of the charge, probably with effect from the implementation date of the Finance Act 2004.

---

3 Stamp Duty Land Tax – Practice Issues, October 2003.
4 Stamp Duty - further information on the changes, issue 6.
5 Sch 15, part 3.

SDLT overview

1.13 The remaining paragraphs of this introduction provide a broad overview of SDLT. As previously stated, SDLT is in reality a new tax with greater scope than stamp duty and the legislation is worded very differently. However, some of the old stamp duty legislation has been retained in substantially the same form (eg group relief) and other new concepts (eg 'linked transactions') bear some similarities to old stamp duty concepts (eg certificate of value wording). It may well be, therefore, that existing stamp duty case law and Inland Revenue guidance relating to stamp duty could be of relevance in determining the meaning of the new legislative provisions. Nevertheless, as with all new legislation, doubt over interpretation will persist in many areas until adequate clarification is available.

Jurisdictional scope of SDLT

1.14 Unlike stamp duty, SDLT is chargeable whether or not there is an instrument or document recording or implementing the relevant transaction. It is also chargeable wherever in the world any document is executed or transaction deemed to take effect. Neither does it matter where the parties to the particular transaction reside. The key jurisdictional factor is whether or not the transaction relates to land which is situate in the United Kingdom. SDLT will only apply if the land is so situate.[6]

Basis of the charge

1.15 The concept of 'conveyance or transfer on sale' applicable to stamp duty is no longer relevant. Furthermore, fixed duties, certificates of value and the

---

6 Ss 42 and 48.

denoting of counterparts are all abolished and documents no longer need to be stamped to be admissible in evidence. In contrast, SDLT is charged on 'land transactions'.[7] This means an acquisition of an estate, interest, right or power in or over land in the UK or the benefit of an obligation, restriction or condition affecting the value of any such estate, interest, right or power. An acquisition of an interest also includes situations where an interest is created, and also where a person benefits by way of enhancement or enlargement of an existing interest as a consequence of a surrender or release of an interest in land and consideration is given. Further, the variation of an interest in land giving rise to a benefit will also constitute an acquisition by the person so benefiting where consideration is given. There are, however, *exclusions* for certain categories of interest. These include interests or rights held for the purposes of securing the payment of money or performance of obligations (eg a mortgage) and licences to use or occupy land.[8] Certain land transactions also enjoy an *exemption* from the charge to SDLT, such as transactions (other than certain transactions between related parties) where no consideration is paid for the acquisition.[9]

Contracts

1.16 In certain circumstances uncompleted contractual arrangements can give rise to SDLT by reference to the transaction provided for in the contract. This arises where a transaction is 'substantially performed' prior to it being completed. Substantial performance for these purposes means either the purchaser taking possession of the whole, or substantially the whole, of the interest in land (including under a licence) or the purchaser paying a substantial amount of the

---

7 S 42.
8 S 48.
9 S 49 and Sch 3.

consideration prior to completion. Substantial for these purposes is treated as 90% or more of the total consideration. In addition to actual possession of land or property, a purchaser will be regarded as taking possession of the land if it receives, or becomes entitled to receive, rents and profits.[10]

1.17 Where a contractual arrangement has given rise to SDLT and the relevant transaction is subsequently completed, SDLT is only charged by reference to completion to the extent that the tax due is greater than that paid previously by reference to the contract. In most cases no further SDLT will be payable.

Options

1.18 The acquisition of an option by a purchaser from a person granting that option over an interest in land is subject to SDLT on a separate and distinct basis from any acquisition of the underlying interest on exercise of the option but may be a linked transaction.[11]

Exchanges

1.19 Where one party to a property transaction agrees to exchange land for another land interest then, in general, both transfers pursuant to the exchange are treated as being subject to SDLT by reference to the market value of the land interests so exchanged – together, in the case of the more valuable property, with other cash or consideration in kind that is paid for it.[12]

---

10 S 44 and SDLT Manual, para 7950.
11 S 46.
12 S 47.

Rates of tax

1.20 Relevant rates of tax are applied to the chargeable consideration in order to determine the amount of SDLT payable in respect of a given transaction. The rates applicable to consideration (like stamp duty, chargeable on a 'slab' basis) other than rent are set out in table 1A (below).

Table 1A	
Commercial[13] or mixed use	
Relevant consideration	**Rate**
Not more than £150,000	0%
£150,001 to £250,000	1%
£250,001 to £500,000	3%
£500,001 plus	4%
Residential	
Relevant consideration	**Rate**
Not more than £60,000	0%
£60,001 to £250,000	1%
£250,001 to £500,000	3%
£500,001 plus	4%

On premiums paid for leases, the rates of charge are as stated above.[14] However, where the annual rent for the lease exceeds £600 there is no nil rate for the premium.[15]

1.21 Rent payable under leases is charged on a different basis (see table 1B, opposite). This rate is applied to the NPV of the rent payable over the entire term of the lease. A special formula is used to calculate NPV.[16]

---

13 In this book, the term 'commercial' is used in place of 'non-residential' for the sake of simplicity but it should be noted that 'non-residential' is the term used in the legislation.
14 S 55.
15 Sch 5, para 9(2).
16 Sch 5, para 3.

Table 1B	
Commerical or mixed use	
Relevant consideration	**Rate**
Up to £150,000	0%
Excess over £150,000	1%
Residential	
Relevant consideration	**Rate**
Up to £60,000	0%
Excess over £60,000	1%

1.22 In considering which rate of tax will apply to a particular transaction, it is necessary to take into account all 'linked' transactions. Transactions are 'linked' if they 'form part of a single scheme, arrangement or series of transactions between the same vendor or purchaser, or in either case, persons connected with them'.[17]

Subsales

1.23 As a result of late amendments made to the Finance Act 2003, subsale relief has been preserved for SDLT, but only in circumstances where the contracts resulting in the ultimate transfer to the final purchaser are all completed at the same time by that transfer. Furthermore, the relief will not apply if any intermediate contract is substantially performed (ie the purchaser takes possession or pays all or substantially all of the purchase price) before completion.[18]

Chargeable consideration

1.24 The basic rule for SDLT is that any consideration in money or money's worth

---

17 S 108.   18 S 45.

given for the subject matter of the transaction, whether directly or indirectly by the purchaser or a person connected with it, will be treated as chargeable consideration. This allows for a range of non-monetary items such as goods and services given in return for a land interest to constitute chargeable consideration. Some of these items, such as services, construction works and debt are specifically provided for, but any other non-monetary consideration is also brought within the general definition of 'consideration in money or money's worth'.[19]

VAT

1.25 Any VAT which is actually chargeable in respect of a sale of a land interest will form part of the chargeable consideration on which SDLT must be calculated. Under the stamp duty regime, VAT always formed part of the chargeable consideration where there was a standard-rated supply or an exempt supply, unless the vendor covenanted not to exercise the option to tax. However, under SDLT, the VAT element should not be taken into account if no VAT is actually charged. Thus, it will be necessary to enquire whether the option to tax has been exercised as regards any transaction involving land which would otherwise be VAT-exempt.[20]

Reverse consideration

1.26 Where a land interest is sold, and the vendor pays the purchaser a premium for it to take the transfer, as with stamp duty, no charge to SDLT will arise on the reverse payment.[21] This also avoids a charge to SDLT arising on transactions

---

19 S 50 and Sch 4.
20 Sch 4, para 2.
21 Sch 4, para 15 and Sch 17A, para 18. Sch 17A was inserted by the Stamp Duty and Stamp Duty Land Tax (Variation of the Finance Act 2003) (No 2) Regulations SI 2003/2816, hereafter termed the 'Variation Regulations'.

such as the grant of a lease, assignment of a lease or surrender of a lease where the payment is to take or take back the land interest.

Transactions involving connected companies

1.27 The SDLT provisions carry over the measures introduced in the Finance Act 2000 which limit the opportunities for planning using connected special purpose vehicles. The provisions impose a market value basis of charge where a vendor transfers or grants a lease of a property to a connected company.[22]

Leasehold obligations

1.28 Certain leasehold obligations can constitute services which will be treated as chargeable consideration. However, in the case of a grant of a lease, most usual obligations (eg to repair, maintain and insure the premises) need not be taken into account.[23]

Contingent, uncertain or unascertained consideration

1.29 The 'contingency principle' which applies to contingent, uncertain or unascertained consideration under stamp duty does not apply to SDLT. Consideration is contingent where it is to be paid or provided, or to cease to be paid or provided, only if some potential future event occurs. A common example of contingent consideration is a further sum becoming payable if the purchaser obtains planning permission.[24]

---

22 S 53.
23 Sch 4, para 13.
24 S 51.

1.30 SDLT is calculated on contingent consideration by assuming the contingent consideration will be paid. A purchaser can apply in certain circumstances to defer the obligation to pay SDLT on the contingent amount until the time the contingency occurs.[25] Once the contingency has occurred, the purchaser is under an obligation to re-examine its liability to SDLT.[26]

1.31 A different rule applies to uncertain or unascertained consideration. Consideration is uncertain where its amount or value varies by reference to future events or performance. Where consideration is uncertain or unascertained, it will be valued on the basis of a reasonable estimate.[27] As with contingent consideration, the taxpayer may need to recalculate the SDLT payable where the consideration becomes certain or is ascertained. This may give rise to a further obligation to pay tax or to a right to a refund.[28] The taxpayer may also be entitled to defer the payment of SDLT in the case of uncertain or contingent consideration.[29]

SDLT on leases

1.32 As with the outgoing stamp duty regime, the SDLT regime imposes a separate charge on the grant of a lease from the charge on the transfer of a freehold or leasehold interest. An entirely different basis of calculation of tax applies to the grant of a lease. The charge to SDLT on rent applies in respect of all chargeable transactions for which the chargeable consideration consists of or includes rent, or where such consideration falls to be taken into account as a linked transaction. The charge to SDLT on rent in relation to a licence to use or occupy land is

---

25 S 90.
26 S 80.
27 S 57.
28 S 80.
29 S 90.

excluded from the category of chargeable interests. Similarly, a tenancy at will is excluded from the new charge.[30]

Basis of tax on leases

1.33 The tax is calculated as a percentage of the NPV of the rent payable over the term of the lease, subject to a temporal discount rate fixed initially at 3.5%. Depending on whether the chargeable interest is residential or commercial, different bands apply (see **table 1B** above).[31]

Rent reviews

1.34 In general, rent reviews and break clauses are ignored in calculating the duty payable on grant, although rent reviews within the first five years of the lease or later abnormal rent reviews can give rise to a further obligation to render a land transaction return and pay further tax.[32] The NPV is calculated on the basis that the same rent is chargeable throughout the term of the lease, unless the lease specifies rental increases at various points (ie a stepped rent). In this case it will be necessary to put into the NPV formula the rent that is payable for each year of the term, but generally specified rent increases after the end of the fifth year will be disregarded.[33]

Agreements for lease

1.35 The legislation contains few provisions specific to agreements for lease, and generally their proper treatment depends on whether there has been completion and/or

---

30 S 48.
31 Sch 5.

32 Sch 17A.
33 Sch 17A, para 7(3).

substantial performance. Thus, no SDLT arises on the entry into an agreement for lease unless the agreement has been substantially performed prior to completion.

Lease variations

1.36 A variation of a lease which has the effect of increasing the amount of rent is treated as a grant of a new lease for the consideration of the additional rent.[34]

Lease surrenders

1.37 In a straightforward situation where a tenant surrenders a lease to a landlord in return for a premium payable by the landlord, the premium will be liable to SDLT at the rates applicable to transfers, ie at the rate of 1, 3 and 4% depending on the size of the premium. However, where a tenant surrenders a lease to a landlord and pays the landlord a premium to take back the lease (a 'reverse surrender'), no SDLT charge will arise.[35]

Surrender and regrants

1.38 The surrender of a lease in return for the grant of a new lease, whether of the same or a different property, will not give rise to SDLT by reference to the market value of either the lease surrendered or the lease granted in return.[36] Where certain requirements are fulfilled and the surrender and regrant relate to substantially the same land, relief is granted such that, during any overlap in the terms of the two leases, SDLT is payable only on the excess of the rents under the new lease.[37]

---

34 Sch 17A, para 13.
35 Sch 17A, para 16.

36 Sch 17A, para 18.
37 Sch 17A, para 9.

Disadvantaged areas relief

1.39 The most important relief in the SDLT code is perhaps the disadvantaged areas relief, which provides a complete exemption from SDLT on commercial property transactions to the extent that the property is in a designated disadvantaged area. Residential property also benefits from the relief, but subject to a cap of £150,000. There are special provisions which set out the distinction between residential and commercial property for these purposes.[38]

Corporate group/reconstruction reliefs

1.40 Existing corporate group/reconstruction reliefs have been incorporated from the current stamp duty legislation in substantially similar form into the SDLT legislation.[39]

Miscellaneous reliefs and exemptions

1.41 There is also provision in the SDLT legislation for a host of targeted specific reliefs and exemptions involving the following areas:

1. charities;
2. grant of certain leases by registered social landlords;
3. transactions in connection with divorce;
4. variation of wills;
5. part-exchange of residential property;
6. relocation relief;

---

38 S 57 and Sch 6.
39 S 62 and Sch 7.

7. compulsory purchase to facilitate development;

8. right to buy transactions and shared ownership leases;

9. certain acquisitions by registered social landlords;

10. alternative financing structures;

11. Private Finance Initiative-funded transactions; and

12. other miscellaneous reliefs.

Claiming reliefs

1.42 Most reliefs must be claimed by filling in the appropriate part of the land transaction return.

Compliance

Paying and filing

1.43 Unlike stamp duty, SDLT is a compulsory tax. Certain land transactions require that a land transaction return ('return') is lodged by a purchaser and that SDLT is paid.[40] The purchaser must self-assess the SDLT payable and the Inland Revenue will take a 'process now, check later' approach to receiving the self-assessment.[41] There is no longer the need to adjudicate the tax payable in order to obtain certain reliefs, nor the option of seeking adjudication in other circumstances to obtain a final figure of the tax which binds the Inland Revenue. That said, a purchaser does have the option of obtaining a pre-transaction or post-transaction ruling from the Inland Revenue.

---

40 S 76.
41 Ss 85 and 86.

Duty to deliver a return

1.44 A return must be delivered by a purchaser to the Inland Revenue in respect of a 'notifiable' transaction within 30 days after the effective date of the transaction.[42] SDLT is payable by the purchaser at the time the return is lodged.[43] Many types of transactions are notifiable, even in certain circumstances where no SDLT is payable. A return needs to be lodged within 30 days of the 'effective date' (which in the case of contracts means when substantial performance occurs, if prior to completion). Not only is the lodgement of a return required in certain instances, but a failure to lodge a return may mean that a purchaser is prevented from registering a land interest with the Land Registry.[44] Further returns may be necessary in certain circumstances, as SDLT can increase or decrease as circumstances change, unlike stamp duty which is paid on a once-and-for-all basis, having regard to a transaction at a particular point in time.

Penalties

1.45 The Inland Revenue has extensive powers to impose interest and penalties including in the case of underpayments of SDLT, failure to lodge returns and failure to comply with directions under the Inland Revenue's information, enquiry and assessment powers. The two most common penalties which a purchaser is likely to encounter are the flat-rate penalty and the tax-related penalty. The flat-rate penalty of £100 is imposed if a return is delivered within three months of the filing date. The penalty rises to £200 for a failure to lodge a return in any other

---

42 S 76.
43 Ss 85 and 86.
44 S 79.

case. A purchaser who fails to lodge a return within 12 months after the filing date is liable to a tax-related penalty not exceeding the amount of SDLT payable.[45] There are also penalties which apply to advisers who assist in the completion of an incorrect return.

Exempt transactions

1.46 The following transactions are exempt from SDLT and do not give rise to an obligation to lodge a return:

1. transactions for no consideration;
2. grants of certain leases by registered social landlords;
3. transactions in connection with divorce; and
4. variation of testamentary dispositions.[46]

Amendment, correction or enquiry into a return

1.47 A purchaser may amend a return delivered by it within 12 months of the filing date.[47] The Inland Revenue may also amend a return so as to correct obvious errors or omissions within nine months of the date on which the return was delivered.[48] The Inland Revenue can also enquire into a return if it gives notice to the purchaser of its intention to do so before the end of a nine-month enquiry period.[49]

---

45 Sch 10, paras 3 and 4.
46 Sch 3.
47 Sch 10, para 6.
48 Sch 10, para 7.
49 Sch 10, part 3.

Power to issue an assessment

1.48 In addition to the general right to correct a return the Inland Revenue can in certain circumstances issue an assessment (a discovery assessment) within six years (21 years in the case of fraud or negligence) after the effective date of the transaction where it is discovered that the amount of tax paid is insufficient, or a relief or an amount of tax repaid to a person has been excessive.[50]

Land registration

1.49 In order to register a land interest with the Land Registry, a certificate of compliance with the SDLT code needs to be produced by a purchaser, save in certain limited circumstances. This will either be a certificate given to a purchaser by the Inland Revenue, certifying that a return has been delivered or a self-certificate given by the purchaser to the Land Registry stating that no return is required in circumstances provided for in the legislation.[51]

Record-keeping

1.50 A purchaser which is required to lodge a return must also keep and preserve such records as may be needed to enable it to deliver a return. In general, the records must be preserved for six years. The kinds of records which must be retained include relevant instruments relating to a transaction, plans and the like. A penalty of up to £3,000 can be imposed for each failure to preserve and keep adequate records.[52]

---

50 Sch 10, part 5.
51 S 79.
52 Sch 10, part 2.

2. Key SDLT Concepts

Basic requirements for charge

2.01 The basic elements of the SDLT charge are:

1. chargeable interest;[1]
2. chargeable transaction;[2]
3. chargeable consideration;[3]
4. applicable rates of SDLT;[4]
5. effective date;[5] and
6. a purchaser.[6]

In order to assess the SDLT treatment of a transaction, all these elements need to be considered, ie whether the nature of the interest in land, the transaction, the consideration, etc give rise to an SDLT charge on a purchaser at the applicable rate of SDLT and, if so, when a transaction triggers the SDLT charge.

Chargeable interest

2.02 In order for a land transaction to be chargeable to SDLT, it needs to relate to a 'chargeable interest'. This is defined as 'an estate interest, right or power in or over land' in the UK[7] or the 'benefit of an obligation, restriction or

---

1 S 48(1).
2 S 49.
3 S 50 and Sch 4 (see further **Ch 7** on non-monetary consideration).
4 S 55(2).
5 S 44(3).
6 S 43(4).

7 For the purposes of the tax, the boundary of the UK is the low water mark of every part of the UK which borders the sea. It does not extend to the bed of the territorial sea but piers, jetties and similar structures, with one end attached to the UK will comprise part of the UK.

condition affecting the value of any such estate, interest, right or power' other than an exempt interest.[8] The UK for these purposes comprises England, Wales, Scotland and Northern Ireland but does not include the Channel Islands or the Isle of Man.

2.03 In addition to the usual freehold and leasehold interests, easements, rights of way, *profits a prendre* and restrictive covenants are also all chargeable interests and, therefore, potentially subject to SDLT.

2.04 The principal exempt interests are: security interests (including mortgages); licences to use or occupy land; and tenancies at will.[9] There are various other unusual property interests, such as franchises and manorial rights that are also exempt. While the Variation Regulations[10] define tenancies at will as a lease, the authors understand that they are nevertheless exempt in accordance with s 48(2).

2.05 A 'security interest' is defined as 'an interest or right (other than a rent charge) held for the purpose of securing the payment of money or the performance of any other obligation'.[11] Accordingly, the interest taken by a lender secured on land will not be the subject of a charge to SDLT when transferred.

2.06 A transaction in respect of an exempt interest within the above categories does not give rise to an obligation to lodge a land transaction return or to self-certify, as it is outside the scope of SDLT. (See **Chapter 9** for more details.)

---

8 S 48(1).
9 S 48(2).
10 Sch 17A, para 1.
11 S 48(3).

2.07 Example of chargeable interests:

A local authority grants a long lease of an area in a retail park to a department store. The store grants a concession in the form of a licence to a perfume retailer to operate from a fixed corner of the store and to use a proportion of its warehouse. The perfume retailer is also granted a right of way over the route between the warehouse and the perfume counter. Two security guards occupy nearby flats owned by the department store under a periodic tenancy from year to year.

In this example, the long lease of the store, the right of way and the security guards' flats are all potentially subject to SDLT, but the concession is an exempt interest.[12]

Chargeable transaction

2.08 The following can constitute a chargeable transaction:

- the acquisition of a chargeable interest – this would include the transfer of a freehold or leasehold interest;
- the creation of a chargeable interest – this would include the grant of a lease;
- the surrender or release of a chargeable interest; and
- the variation of a chargeable interest.[13]

2.09 It is important to note how wide the scope of the SDLT charge can be. A release by a landlord of the tenant's obligations under a lease or just an individual restrictive covenant is a chargeable transaction.[14]

---

12 If the flats are rented to the security guards for nil rent there would most likely be a charge to SDLT on the deemed benefit if provided by reason of employment. See **Ch 7**.
13 S 43(3).
14 Also included are transactions involving equitable interests, easements and options.

Chargeable consideration

2.10 The basic rule for SDLT is that any consideration in money or money's worth given for the subject matter of the transaction directly or indirectly by the purchaser or a person connected with it will be treated as chargeable consideration.[15] So far as the person providing the consideration is concerned, this is actually a narrower basis than the stamp duty charge, which imposed a charge on stampable documents irrespective of who provided the consideration. This allows for a range of non-monetary items, such as goods and services given in return for a land interest, to constitute chargeable consideration. Some of these items, such as services,[16] construction works[17] and debt[18] are specifically provided for, but there may be other items which are brought within the general definition of 'consideration in money or money's worth'. This is dealt with in more detail in **Chapter 7.**

2.11 Consideration attributed to fixtures and fittings[19] is regarded as chargeable, but consideration attributed to any other items such as chattels, goodwill, stock, intellectual property or motor vehicles is disregarded. For further guidance see Stamp Duty Information Bulletin – Issue 6, which is included in the CD-Rom accompanying this book.

2.12 A further issue is the apportionment of consideration. The legislation states in Schedule 4, paragraph 4 that the principle of just and reasonable

---

15 Sch 4, para 1(1).
16 Sch 4, para 11.
17 Sch 4, para 10.
18 Sch 4, para 8.
19 The degree and purpose of annexation is relevant to whether an item will be treated as a fixture. See **para 13.14**.

apportionment should be applied for the purposes of attributing consideration: a) between two or more land transactions; b) between a land transaction and another matter; and c) as between matters in relation to which the consideration is not chargeable. Any attribution which is not just and reasonable will be disregarded. For example, where two plots of land are purchased, one of which benefits from disadvantaged area relief and the other does not, an attempt to exaggerate the amount of consideration attributed to the plot within the disadvantaged area will not reduce the SDLT liability. Similarly, if both land and other assets are being sold, tax cannot be saved by attributing more than a just and reasonable amount of the consideration to the non-chargeable assets. For the purpose of the attribution of consideration, the legislation aggregates all consideration and all transactions that are part of 'the same bargain' to prevent the ring-fencing of consideration by separating transactions or expressing consideration to be payable for different items.

2.13 Example:

A Ltd wishes to sell a restaurant business to B Ltd consisting of a lease, goodwill including a business name, certain furniture and stock. Installed in the restaurant is an air-conditioning system. The consideration genuinely attributable to the goodwill, furniture and stock will not form part of the consideration chargeable to SDLT. Attributing consideration to the air conditioning will not reduce the SDLT payable as this is a fixture.

Rates of tax

2.14 For the rates of tax which are applicable generally, see **para 3.36** and for the rates of tax applying to consideration which is rent, see **para 5.58**.

Effective date of transaction

2.15 When does the charge to SDLT arise? This depends on the 'effective date of the transaction'. The basic rule is that the effective date is the completion of the transaction,[20] but this may be earlier if, broadly speaking, the price is paid earlier or the purchaser goes into occupation earlier.[21] The effective date must be inserted in Box 4 of the land transaction return. The effective date of a transaction is the material date for the SDLT liability to arise, and from which 30 days are given for a land transaction return to be lodged at the Inland Revenue together with the tax.[22]

2.16 A contract (which in this chapter includes both a contract for sale and an agreement for lease) to sell or grant a chargeable interest does not give rise to a charge to SDLT until it is completed, which is the effective date. When a transaction is completed, the charge to SDLT arises and the contract and the transaction on completion are treated as a single land transaction.[23] However, if the contract has already been substantially performed before completion, then a separate charge to SDLT arises at the date of substantial performance of the contract.[24] As mentioned below at **para 2.29**, a further land transaction will take place when the contract is completed.[25]

Substantial performance

2.17 A contract *can* give rise to a charge to SDLT at the date of substantial performance even if completion has not taken place. This is one of the key measures

---

20 S 44(3).
21 S 44(4).
22 Ss 76(1) and 86(1).
23 S 44(3).
24 S 44(4).
25 S 44(8).

in the SDLT regime aimed at preventing avoidance by 'resting on contract'. A contract, even a conditional contract, can also give rise to an SDLT liability if it has been substantially performed.[26] For example, a business sale which includes a leasehold interest may be conditional on a landlord's consent to assignment. The contract to assign may be substantially performed if the purchaser goes into possession, for example, on entry into the business sale agreement before the agreement to assign becomes unconditional.

2.18 A contract is substantially performed where either:

1. a substantial amount of the consideration is paid or provided ('early consideration'); or
2. the purchaser or a person connected with the purchaser takes possession of the whole, or substantially the whole of the subject-matter of the contract ('early possession').[27]

Early consideration

2.19 Consideration will be paid early when:

1. 90% or more of the consideration is paid or provided; or
2. a payment of rent is made.[28]

2.20 The SDLT Manual[29] clarifies that 'a substantial amount of the consideration' will be 90% or more of the total consideration payable. Therefore, where at the

---

26 SDLT Manual, para 00880.
27 S 44(5).
28 S 44(7).
29 Para 7950.

time of exchange of contracts a deposit of 10% of the consideration is paid, this will not constitute substantial performance of the contract and thus will not yet give rise to a liability to SDLT. The SDLT Manual further clarifies that the 90% rule will not apply to prevent substantial performance where the circumstances of the transaction are such that, in substance, the whole of the consideration has in fact been provided. It gives the example of a contract providing for the purchase of a property with a market value of £10m for a total consideration of £15m, £10m payable in 2004 and the remainder in 2099. In these circumstances, the transaction will be regarded as already having been substantially performed.

2.21 If a deposit of 90% or more of the consideration is paid and held under a contract on an agency basis, it is the authors' view that this would most likely constitute substantial performance of the contract. If such a deposit was paid and held on a stakeholder basis, the position is less clear. The vendor would not be entitled to access the deposit moneys and therefore the purchaser may not be considered to have paid or provided the consideration. There may nevertheless be an argument that, even in this scenario, the consideration has been provided by the purchaser.

2.22 As a result of the substantial performance condition, it will not be possible to avoid a charge to SDLT by the parties entering into a contract for sale and purchase, and the purchaser paying the purchase price without taking a transfer (known under stamp duty as 'resting on contract'). Under SDLT, as soon as a substantial amount of the purchase price is paid, the transaction becomes liable to SDLT.

2.23 Where the only consideration is rent, substantial performance will occur when the first payment of rent is made if this is before completion.[30] If the

---

30 S 44(7)(b).

consideration for a land transaction consists of both rent and other consideration, substantial performance will occur on the earlier of either the occasion when 90% of the non-rent consideration is paid or when the first payment of rent is made.[31]

Early possession

2.24 Possession will be taken early when:

1. a person takes physical possession of the land; or
2. a person receives or becomes entitled to receive rents and profits.

2.25 The taking of physical possession will constitute substantial performance, such as where the purchaser goes into occupation or moves, for example, plant or equipment onto the site. It is immaterial whether the possession is taken under the contract itself or under a licence or lease of a temporary character.[32] It should be noted that while a licence is an exempt interest, a contract (eg an agreement for lease) can be substantially performed by possession pursuant to a licence, with the result that the periodic payments under the licence become chargeable to SDLT. This means that in the common situation where a tenant, or a building company at the tenant's order, enters the site early under a licence in order to carry out works, substantial performance will already have taken place. The authors consider that wherever the builder is commissioned by the tenant, the same conclusion may apply, even if the works are solely for the benefit of the landlord. The SDLT Manual[33] states that the commencement of fitting-out works will constitute the taking of possession if the trade commences once the fitting-out works are completed. The authors understand that this does not mean that

---

31 S 44(7)(c). **33** Para 7900a.
32 S 44(6).

substantial performance is deemed not to have occurred if there is a hiatus between the time the works are completed and the tenant's trade commences. However, if the vendor takes back occupation of the land after the building works, this would show that the vendor is still in control of the land and that the purchaser had not yet taken possession and in the circumstances such possession would be ignored.

2.26 A further issue is what happens where the purchaser goes into physical possession but only occupies a small part of the building. In these circumstances, it might be said that the purchaser had not taken possession of 'substantially the whole' of the subject matter of the contract. The authors understand that the question of substantial performance will require an examination of the factual background. Thus if the vendor still owns and bears the risk of the remainder of the land, the purchaser may not have taken possession. For example, if the vendor still provides a fence and security for the land during the course of construction, this may indicate that, even though the purchaser is occupying part of it, the land is still effectively controlled by the vendor. In contrast, if it is only due to a lack of resources that the builder is carrying out works to part of the land, this may show that the purchaser has in fact taken possession. The 90% guideline as regards the meaning of 'substantially the whole' may also be helpful in this context, but it should be emphasised that this is not a hard and fast rule.

2.27 In order for there to be substantial performance, there needs to be a contract which can be substantially performed. Where there is no contract and a tenant has been allowed into possession before the lease is signed, the lease will not have been substantially performed, but some other interest such as a licence or tenancy at will may have been granted.

2.28 A purchaser will be regarded as taking possession of the whole, or substantially the whole, of the subject matter of the contract once in receipt of rents and profits or once it has obtained the right to receive them.[34] For example, the receipt of rents and profits could give rise to an early effective date where a contract is not completed for some months, but it is agreed that the purchaser is entitled to rents on an occupational lease from the first quarter-day after contract. The mere apportionment of rent, even if the date of apportionment precedes completion, does not give rise to an early date of substantial performance.

Completion after substantial performance

2.29 Where a contract has been substantially performed, giving rise to an effective date prior to completion, this will not be the end of the matter. The substantial performance of the contract is the first notifiable land transaction. The completion of the contract by a conveyance or lease will constitute a further notifiable land transaction,[35] and SDLT will need to be paid on that second land transaction to the extent that the tax payable exceeds that on the earlier land transaction. Even if the consideration payable on completion is identical to the contractual consideration, two land transaction returns will need to be submitted, one within 30 days of substantial performance of the contract and another within 30 days of completion.[36] The Inland Revenue has initiated a special procedure whereby the second land transaction return is submitted to Manchester Stamp Office, which intervenes to prevent SDLT being charged twice. See **para 14.56** for more details.

---

34 S 44(6).
35 S 44(8).
36 SDLT Manual, para 00890.

2.30 Where a contract has been substantially performed but is later rescinded, annulled or otherwise not carried into effect, any tax paid by virtue of substantial performance can be reclaimed from the Inland Revenue by submission of an amended land transaction return.[37] The legislation does not give the Inland Revenue discretion to refuse such a repayment of SDLT. Where the contract is only partially rescinded, annulled or otherwise not carried into effect, a partial refund will be made. Thus, if a contract relating to two plots of land is substantially performed by the purchaser paying 90% or more of the purchase consideration and SDLT is paid as required, if the contract is then varied so that only one plot is subject to the sale, the tax attributable to the consideration relating to the other plot may be reclaimed.

Purchaser liability

2.31 Unlike stamp duty, the new SDLT charge is mandatory and is not a voluntary charge paid by whichever party requires a stampable document to be enforced or registered at the Land Registry. The purchaser is the person who is liable to pay the tax,[38] and it is the purchaser, (and not any other person, even its agent),[39] who signs the land transaction return and thus takes responsibility for the declarations it contains.[40] Clearly, in certain circumstances and depending on the bargaining position of the parties, the vendor and purchaser may agree for some sharing of the SDLT liability, but it is the purchaser who must pay the tax and deliver a land transaction return within the time limits to avoid interest and penalties,[41] however such liability is funded. A person who acquires a chargeable interest will only be treated as a purchaser and thus

---

37 S 44(9).
38 S 85(1).
39 But see **para 14.79** regarding powers
of attorney.

40 Sch 10, para 1.
41 S 85(1).

liable for SDLT if they have either provided consideration or are a party to the transaction.[42] This is to prevent third parties being treated as purchasers and held liable for SDLT on the grounds that a right over land of theirs may benefit from a land transaction.

2.32 The liability of different types of purchasers, such as joint purchasers, trusts and partners is discussed in **paras 14.07-34**.

Distinction between residential and commercial property

2.33 The distinction between residential and commercial property[43] is relevant to two matters:

1. the thresholds for the minimum rate of SDLT; and
2. the form of disadvantaged area relief which may apply.

The application of the distinction is discussed further in **Chapter 9**.

2.34 'Residential property' means:[44]

1. a building that is used or is suitable for use as a dwelling, or is in the process of being constructed or being adapted for such use; and
2. land that is or forms part of the garden or grounds of such a building, including any building or structure on that land.

---

42 S 43(5).
43 As mentioned in **Ch 1**, in this book the term 'commercial' is used in place of 'non-residential' for the sake of simplicity but it should be noted that 'non-residential' is the term used in the legislation.
44 S 116(1).

Interests in or rights over land that exist for the benefit of buildings within the definition above are also regarded as 'residential property'. However, where a dwelling which would otherwise be regarded as 'residential property' is one of six or more separate dwellings which are the subject of a single transaction involving the transfer or grant of a lease in respect of that land, all those dwellings are regarded as commercial property.[45]

2.35 The legislation specifically deems buildings used for the following purposes to be 'used as a dwelling':[46]

- residential accommodation for school pupils;
- residential accommodation for students who are not school pupils;
- residential accommodation for members of the armed forces; and
- an institution that is the sole or main residence of at least 90% of its residents.

2.36 The legislation also contains a list of building uses which are deemed not to be 'used as a dwelling'.[47] These are as follows:

- a home or other institution providing residential accommodation for children;
- a hall of residence for students in further or higher education;
- a home or other institution providing residential accommodation with personal care for persons in need of care by reason of old age, disablement, past or present dependence on alcohol or drugs or past or present mental disorder;
- a hospital or hospice;

---

45 S 116(7).
46 S 116(2).
47 S 116(3).

- a prison or similar establishment; and

- a hotel or similar establishment.

All other land, including bare land,[48] is regarded as commercial.

Linked transactions

2.37 In assessing the appropriate rate of tax in respect of a chargeable transaction, it is necessary to take into account the consideration passing under any linked transactions.[49] Transactions are linked if they 'form part of a single scheme, arrangement or series of transactions between the same vendor or purchaser or, in either case, persons connected with them'.[50] This test is somewhat wider than the stamp duty test for certificate of value purposes, as it includes a 'scheme or arrangement'. For this reason, where two transactions are entered into between the same parties, the device of entering into legally separate agreements, of itself, would not prevent the transactions being linked transactions.

2.38 There is case law and practice in relation to the meaning of 'series of transactions' under the old stamp duty regime, and this may be useful in an SDLT context:

- *Attorney-General v Cohen*[51] – where several properties are purchased from the same vendor by the same person at the same auction in separate lots, they do not form part of a series of transactions. The transactions were not viewed as

---

48 Statement of Practice SP1/03, para 28.
49 S 55(4)(b).
50 S 108(1).
51 [1937] 1 KB 478.

linked in that case because there was no contractual link between the different purchases – the link was merely fortuitous.

- *Kimbers & Co v IRC*[52] – provided the transactions are legally independent (in this case the second transaction was not a sale but a construction contract), the transactions will not be viewed as linked, even where the parties are the same and the parties would not have entered into any of the transactions without all the other transactions being entered into.[53] This principle is likely to be disapplied for SDLT purposes. The fact that, for example, one transaction is a transfer and the other is the grant of a lease will not assist, as SDLT focuses on transactions rather than their legal form. This case is also taken as authority for an enforceability test, ie whether one contract can be enforced without the other. See also *Paul v IRC*.[54]

2.39 Under the existing stamp duty case law and guidance, for transactions to be linked, it is not enough that sequential transactions are entered into between the same parties or connected parties of the other potentially linked transactions. It is necessary that there is some interdependence linking the transactions. For example, where an option is granted in respect of land for a substantial consideration and the option is later exercised for further consideration, it cannot be said that the later land transaction could be effected without the first, and thus in most cases they would be regarded as linked, as is recognised by the legislation.[55] Similarly, where a landlord grants on the same day a lease of two neighbouring units on identical terms, one to a tenant and another either to the same tenant or to another company

---

52 [1936] 1 KB 132.
53 The building contract was construed as coming into operation only after completion of the sale.
54 See also *Paul v IRC* [1936] SC 443.
55 S 46.

in the tenant's group, there would be obvious interdependence linking the transactions. However, any subsequent renewal of the leases at the same time would not necessarily be regarded as linked transactions. Where the vendor and purchaser under the transactions are not the same and are not connected parties and the vendor and purchaser of the first transaction are a party to the second transaction, there should not be a risk of the transactions being linked. Where the conveyance or lease under each of the transactions is pursuant to the same contract and between the same parties, there will be little doubt that the transactions are linked.

2.40 The additional words 'scheme' and 'arrangement', which were not present within the stamp duty definition of linked transactions, are similar to those used in several anti-avoidance provisions in the stamp duty group relief context and in direct tax legislation. While, at the time of writing, there is no guidance on how they will be applied in the SDLT context, on the assumption that the guidance in Inland Revenue Statement of Practice SP3/98 applies, 'arrangements' will likely include not only the contractual linkage of transactions or their interconditionality, but also where there is some understanding between the parties that both or all of the transactions are to take place. An understanding of one party to the transaction is not sufficient – the understanding needs to be bilateral in order to constitute an 'arrangement'. The understanding must be not just a proposal, but an understanding that there is a strong likelihood that the transactions would be pursued together. However, there is no need for the understanding to be documented in any way, for example, in heads of terms. The term 'scheme' is not generally known in Inland Revenue guidance, and it is difficult to interpret, though it may bear a similar meaning to 'arrangements'.

2.41 The comments above on linked transactions give rise to few clear-cut rules and such rules as there are may not have the same application in an SDLT context. However, one point is clear, that in an SDLT context, if the parties are wholly different (including any connected parties), the other transaction should not be linked. Other than this, in many cases, pending guidance from the Inland Revenue, it will be difficult to plan a transaction in complete confidence on the issue of linked transactions as, for example, it will no longer be sufficient to show that the transactions are legally independent. Further, the impact of the leading stamp duty case on building works, *Prudential v IRC*[56] in an SDLT context is in the process of being considered by the Inland Revenue and the result of this may have some bearing on the meaning of 'linked transactions'.

2.42 In addition to the issue of linked transactions, which is mainly relevant to the application of the SDLT bands of tax, the 'just and reasonable apportionment' principle mentioned at **para 2.12** above has relevance as regards the amount of consideration which is taken into account. The concept of 'a single bargain' in that context should therefore be considered alongside the 'linked transactions' issue in assessing the SDLT liability of a proposed transaction or set of transactions.

Major interest in land

2.43 The concept of 'major interest' is used in many places throughout the SDLT regime, such as in relation to exchanges of land, and is crucial to determining when a land transaction is notifiable to the Inland Revenue.[57] It is also a require-ment for a number of reliefs, such as in relation to exchanges of residential land with housebuilders and associated reliefs, relocation relief and other reliefs relat-ing to acquisitions of residential property. In England and Wales a freehold or a

---

56 [1992] STC 863.
57 S 117.

leasehold interest, whether legal or equitable, will be regarded as a major interest. Different interests will constitute a major interest in Scotland and Northern Ireland.

Contingent, uncertain and unascertained consideration

2.44 It is particularly important in the SDLT context to identify whether the consideration is contingent, uncertain or unascertained, as this will have ramifications for the calculation of the tax, the filing of returns, future monitoring of adjustments to the consideration and the possibility of deferring payment of some of the SDLT liability. The rules applicable to contingent, uncertain or unascertained consideration are different depending on whether the consideration in question is rent consideration or non-rent, and for this reason the basis of assessment of contingent, uncertain and unascertained consideration is set out in the chapters dealing with the sale of a freehold and a leasehold interest and the grant of a lease. The points in this chapter are aimed to assist in identifying when contingent, uncertain or unascertained consideration is in question.

2.45 The contingency principle which applied to contingent, uncertain or unascertained consideration under stamp duty does not apply to SDLT. The principle allowed stamp duty to be calculated by reference to a *'prima facie* sum', eg a minimum amount where the consideration was stated to be subject to a minimum. SDLT introduces a new method for calculating tax payable on contingent, uncertain or unascertained consideration and also gives a purchaser the opportunity to delay payment of SDLT in certain instances. The new principle applies a different rule for contingent consideration to the one applying for uncertain and unascertained consideration. As regards contingent consideration, at the effective date of the transaction, it is necessary to bring into account the maximum consideration that would be payable, whether that assumes that the contingency does occur or that it does not occur. As regards uncertain and unascertained consideration, the rule is that the total consideration for the transaction must be estimated, which involves a forecast of the likely result of whichever events will cause the uncertain or unascertained consideration to become certain or ascertained. Depending on whether the land transaction is a sale or the grant of a lease, different rules apply regarding the timing of reassessments of the consideration in view of the consideration ceasing to be contingent, uncertain or unascertained. Further details of these rules are contained in **Chapters 3** and **5**.

Contingent consideration

2.46 Consideration is contingent where it is to be paid or provided, or will cease to be paid or provided, only if some uncertain future event occurs.[58] For example, a person agrees to sell a freehold interest in a vacant plot of land for an upfront payment of £100,000 and a further payment of £500,000 if the purchaser obtains planning permission to develop the land within two years of sale. Alternatively, the plot of land might be sold for £600,000, with £500,000 of that sum held in escrow until two years from the sale, to be returned to the purchaser if planning permission is not obtained by that date.

Uncertain or unascertained consideration

2.47 Consideration is uncertain where its amount or value depends on uncertain future events.[59] The legislation does not define unascertained consideration but the authors understand this to mean consideration that is not dependent on future

---

58 S 51(3).
59 S 51(3).

events but nevertheless remains undetermined at the effective date of the transaction. An example of uncertain consideration is where a lease is granted for an annual rent which includes a fixed element plus a variable element set at a percentage of the income from sub-lettings. The variable element is uncertain, as it depends on events following the effective date of the transaction. Another example is where a lease is granted of a shop for an annual rent which includes a fixed element, plus a further element based on the turnover of an occupying clothes retail business as appearing in turnover accounts prepared from year to year. An example of unascertained consideration is where land is sold for consideration based on profits in accounts relating to a period before the effective date of the transaction, and which have yet to be drawn up.

3. SALE OF FREEHOLD

3.01 In order for a transaction to fall within the charge to SDLT, it needs to constitute a 'land transaction'.[1] The sale of a freehold interest is a chargeable 'land transaction' as it is a transaction where the subject matter is a 'chargeable interest'. There is no definition of 'freehold' for SDLT purposes, but any interest which is 'an estate, interest, right or power in or over land' in the UK[2] will constitute a chargeable interest.

Sale of freehold – checklist
(a) At what point do I need to consider SDLT (see **para 3.02**)?
(b) Is the property in a disadvantaged area (see **para 3.18**)?
(c) Does any other relief apply (see **para 3.19**)?
(d) Is there any other planning I can do (see **para 3.20**)?
(e) What is the chargeable consideration (see **para 3.21**)?
(i)   Do I take into account VAT (see **para 3.22**)?
(ii)   Is there any non-monetary consideration (see **para 3.23**)?
(iii) Is the consideration contingent, uncertain or unascertained (see **para 3.24**)?
(f) What rate of SDLT applies (see **para 3.36**)?
(g) How do I account for SDLT (see **para 3.37**)?
(h) Is any ongoing compliance necessary (see **para 3.38**)?

At what point do I need to consider SDLT?

3.02 When does the charge to SDLT arise? This depends on the 'effective date of the transaction'. The basic rule is that the effective date is the completion of the

---

1 S 43(1).
2 S 48(1).

transaction,[3] but this may be earlier if, broadly speaking, the price is paid earlier or the purchaser goes into occupation earlier.[4] For further details see **paras 2.15** and **2.16**.

3.03 A contract to sell a freehold interest does not generally give rise to a charge to SDLT until it is completed, which is the effective date. When a transaction is completed the charge to SDLT arises and the contract and the transaction on completion are treated as a single land transaction.[5] However, if the contract has already been substantially performed before completion, then the charge to SDLT will be the date of substantial performance when the charge to SDLT arises.[6]

Substantial performance

3.04 A contract *can* give rise to a charge to SDLT at the date of substantial performance even if no completion has taken place. This is one of the key measures in the SDLT regime aimed at preventing avoidance by 'resting on contract'. A contract, even a conditional contract, can also give rise to an SDLT liability if it has been substantially performed.[7]

3.05 A contract for the sale of a freehold interest is substantially performed where either:

1. a substantial amount of the consideration is paid or provided ('early consideration'); or

---

3 S 44(3).
4 S 44(5).
5 S 44(3).
6 S 44(4).
7 SDLT Manual, para 00880.

2.   the purchaser or a person connected with the purchaser takes possession of the whole, or substantially the whole of the subject matter of the contract 'early possession'.[8]

Early consideration

3.06 In the context of a contract for sale of a freehold interest, consideration will be paid early when 90% or more of the consideration is paid or provided.

3.07 The Inland Revenue SDLT Manual[9] clarifies that 'a substantial amount of the consideration' will be 90% or more of the total consideration payable. Therefore where at the time of exchange of contracts a deposit of 10% of the consideration is paid, this will not constitute substantial performance of the contract and thus will not yet give rise to a liability to SDLT. The SDLT Manual further clarifies that the 90% rule will not apply where the circumstances of the transaction are such that in substance the whole of the consideration has in fact been provided. It gives the example of a contract providing for the purchase of a property with a market value of £10m for a total consideration of £15m, £10m payable in 2004 and the remainder in 2099. In these circumstances the transaction will be regarded as already having been substantially performed.

3.08 If a deposit of 90% or more of the consideration is paid and held under a contract on an agency basis, it is the authors' view that this would most likely constitute substantial performance of the contract. If such a deposit was paid and held on a stakeholder basis, in the authors' view the position is less clear. The vendor would not be entitled to access the deposit moneys and therefore the purchaser

---

8 S 44(5).
9 Para 00880.

may not be considered to have paid or provided the consideration. There may nevertheless be an argument that, even in this scenario, the consideration has been provided by the purchaser.

3.09 As a result of the substantial performance condition, it will not be possible to avoid a charge to SDLT by the parties entering into a contract for sale and purchase, and the purchaser paying the purchase price without taking a transfer ('resting on contract'). Under SDLT, as soon as a substantial amount of the purchase price is paid, the transaction becomes liable to SDLT.

Early possession

3.10 Possession in the case of a sale of a freehold interest will be taken early when:

1.   a person takes physical possession of the land; or
2.   a person receives or becomes entitled to receive rents and profits.

3.11 The taking of physical possession will constitute substantial performance, such as where the purchaser goes into occupation or moves, for example, plant or equipment on to the site. It is immaterial whether the possession is taken under the contract itself or under a licence or lease (eg from the vendor) of a temporary character.[10] The authors understand that the issue of taking possession as a question of fact, and much will rest on whether the vendor is still enjoying the benefit and taking the risk in relation to the land. If the vendor takes back occupation of the land after initial access by the purchaser this would show that the vendor is still in control of the land and that the purchaser had not yet taken possession.

---

10 S 44(6).

3.12 A further issue is what happens where the purchaser goes into physical possession but only occupies a small part of the building. In these circumstances it might be said that the purchaser had not taken possession of 'substantially the whole' of the subject matter of the contract. If the vendor still owns and bears the risk of the remainder of the land, the purchaser may not have taken possession. For example, if the vendor still provides a fence and security for the land during the course of construction, this may indicate that even though the purchaser is occupying part, the land is still effectively controlled by the vendor. If it is only due to a lack of resources that the builder is only carrying out works to part of the land, this may show that the purchaser has in fact taken possession. The 90% guideline as regards the meaning of 'substantially the whole' may also be used in this context, but it should be emphasised that this is not a hard and fast rule.

3.13 In order for there to be substantial performance, there needs to be a contract which can be substantially performed. In the case of freehold sales, it would be rare that a purchaser is allowed into possession without a contract, and thus the question of whether there has been early substantial performance will generally need to be considered whenever the purchaser gains early access.

3.14 A purchaser of a freehold interest subject to a lease or leases will be regarded as taking possession of the whole, or substantially the whole of the subject matter of the contract once in receipt of rents and profits, or once it has obtained the right to receive them.[11] For example, the receipt of rents and profits could give rise to an early effective date where a contract is not completed for some months but it is agreed that the purchaser is entitled to rents on an occupational lease from the first quarter day after contract. The mere apportionment of rent, even if the

---

11 S 44(6).

date of apportionment precedes completion, does not give rise to an early date of substantial performance.

Completion after substantial performance

3.15 Where a contract has been substantially performed, giving rise to an effective date prior to completion, this will not be the end of the matter. The substantial performance of the contract is the first notifiable land transaction.[12] The completion of the contract by a conveyance will constitute a further notifiable land transaction, and SDLT will need to be paid on that second land transaction to the extent that the tax payable exceeds the tax payable on the earlier land transaction. Even if the consideration payable on completion is identical to the contractual consideration, two land transaction returns will need to be submitted, one within 30 days of substantial performance of the contract and another within 30 days of completion.[13] The Inland Revenue has initiated a special procedure whereby the second land transaction return is submitted to the Manchester Stamp Office, which intervenes to prevent SDLT being charged twice (see **para 14.56**).

3.16 Where a contract has been substantially performed but is later rescinded, annulled or otherwise not carried into effect, any tax paid by virtue of substantial performance can be reclaimed from the Inland Revenue by submission of an amended land transaction return. The legislation does not give the Inland Revenue discretion to refuse such a repayment of SDLT. Where the contract is only partially rescinded, annulled or otherwise not carried into effect, a partial refund will be made. Thus if a contract relating to two plots of land is substantially performed by the purchaser paying 90% or more of the purchase consideration and SDLT is paid

---

12 S 44(8).
13 SDLT Manual, para 00890.

as required, if the contract is then varied so that only one plot is subject to the sale, the tax attributable to the consideration relating to the other plot may be reclaimed.

3.17 A particular question arises in the context of a tenant who enters into a contract to acquire the reversion (ie the freehold) from the landlord. In these circumstances the authors understand that the question is when the tenant commences occupation pursuant to the reversion, as opposed to the lease. For example, if the landlord releases the tenant from paying rent and/or observing the covenants in the lease early, this may indicate that the tenant is occupying pursuant to the reversion and thus will have substantially performed the contract relating to the reversion.

Is the property in a disadvantaged area?

3.18 Since no SDLT is payable in relation to commercial property and low-value residential land in disadvantaged areas, it is always necessary to check whether land is in a disadvantaged area. Some surprising areas are regarded as disadvantaged, such as Canary Wharf in London (see **Chapter 9**).

Does any other relief apply?

3.19 You should always consider whether reliefs are available, which are generally claimed on the land transaction return and not by adjudication (see **Chapter 9**).

Is there any other planning I can do?

3.20 There are various steps which a purchaser might take to mitigate SDLT liability, such as use of partnerships, unit trusts, property owning companies and legitimate apportionments of consideration (see **Chapter 13**).

What is the chargeable consideration?

3.21 Any consideration in money or money's worth will constitute chargeable consideration. Thus consideration consisting of works or services provided by the purchaser may constitute the consideration, or additional consideration for the land transaction (see **Chapter 7**).

Do I take into account VAT?

3.22 Any VAT which is actually chargeable on a sale of a freehold interest will form part of the chargeable consideration on which SDLT must be calculated.[14] Under the stamp duty regime VAT always formed part of the chargeable consideration where there was a standard-rated supply or an exempt supply *unless* the vendor covenanted not to exercise the option to tax. Under SDLT, the VAT element is only taken into account if VAT is actually charged. Thus it will be necessary to enquire whether the option to tax has been exercised as regards any transaction involving land which is VAT-exempt. A VAT election *after* the effective date of the transaction is disregarded and is not treated as deferred consideration for the transaction. Where VAT forms part of the chargeable consideration, this amount is included in the figure in Box 10 and the VAT amount should be inserted in Box 11 of the land transaction return.

---

14 Sch 4, para 2.

Is there any non-monetary consideration?

3.23 See **Chapter 7** below regarding non-monetary consideration and **paras 3.41-3.47** below regarding exchanges.

Is the consideration contingent, uncertain or unascertained?

3.24 Refer to **paras 2.44-2.47** for the discussion of what constitutes contingent, uncertain and unascertained consideration. It is possible to defer payment of SDLT in relation to contingent and uncertain consideration (see **Chapter 14**) but not consideration that is unascertained.

3.25 Two rules apply, one to contingent consideration, the other to uncertain and unascertained consideration:

3.26 *Contingent consideration* – the amount or value of the consideration is determined on the assumption that the outcome of the contingency will be such that the consideration is payable or, as the case may be does not cease to be payable.[15]

3.27 Accordingly, if the consideration would increase as a result of the contingency happening, the return due on the effective date of the transaction must calculate SDLT by reference to the higher amount of consideration that would be payable. If the consideration would be reduced as a result of a contingency happening, then SDLT is calculated by reference to the amount of consideration payable had the contingency not happened.

---

15 S 51(1).

3.28 When the contingency occurs, or it becomes clear that it will not occur, if additional tax is payable, or tax is payable when none was payable before (eg if the additional consideration takes the transaction over an exempt threshold) then a revised return must be submitted within 30 days of that event together with the extra tax payable, applying the same rates of tax as applied at the effective date of the transaction.[16] If, as a result of the contingency, or it becoming clear that it will not occur, less tax is payable, the amount overpaid may be reclaimed from the Inland Revenue with interest calculated from the date the overpayment was made.[17]

3.29 Example:

A plot of land is sold for a consideration of £1m with a further £500,000 being payable if and when planning permission is granted for the construction of a block of flats on the land. Within 30 days of the effective date, a return must be filed with SDLT calculated on £1.5m. If planning permission is granted, no further land transaction return will be required. If planning permission is refused, a revised land transaction return may be submitted on that event to reclaim SDLT paid on the £500,000. Had the sale been for a consideration of £1.5m with the proviso that if a pending planning application was refused the vendor would return £500,000 to the purchaser, the consideration for SDLT purposes would nevertheless be £1.5m. If planning permission is granted, no further land transaction return is required. If planning permission is refused, a revised land transaction return may be submitted in order to reclaim SDLT calculated on the £500,000.

3.30 *Uncertain and unascertained consideration* – by contrast to contingent consideration, where there is a sale for uncertain or unascertained consideration, the SDLT payable on the effective date of the transaction must be calculated on the basis

---

16 S 80(2).
17 S 80(4).

of a 'reasonable estimate' of the amount or value of the consideration.[18] However, this is not the end of the matter. When an event occurs which makes the consideration payable certain or ascertained, as the case may be, a revised land transaction return must be submitted if the 'reasonable estimate' proves to be an underestimate.[19] If the 'reasonable estimate' proves to be an overestimate then a revised land transaction may be submitted in order to make a claim for a refund of the overpayment together with interest from the effective date of the transaction.

3.31 In the case of the sale of a freehold interest, there is a right to request deferral of payment of the SDLT payable in relation to contingent or uncertain consideration, but not in relation to consideration which consists of only unascertained consideration.[20]

3.32 In the case of freehold sales, a typical example of uncertain consideration is where the sale agreement provides for further consideration to be payable in the form of an overage element, dependent, for example on income from lettings.

3.33 In such a situation, the overage element will need to be estimated at the time of the sale. SDLT will be payable at the time of the sale calculated both on the consideration payable on completion and a reasonable estimate of the total of the overage element.[21] It may be possible to defer payment of the uncertain element of the consideration using the procedure in the Administration Regulations[22] (see **Chapter 14**).

3.34 Unless the original estimate proves to be correct, a further land transaction return will need to be submitted within 30 days of the overage being determined

---

18 S 51(2).
19 S 80(2).
20 S 90(1).

21 S 51(2).
22 Stamp Duty Land Tax (Administration) Regulations, SI 2003/2837.

containing a revised figure of the total chargeable consideration for the transaction together with the additional SDLT payable.[23] There may be several events that cause an uncertain amount to be determined, in which case a revised return may be necessary following the occurrence of each of these events. This is to be contrasted with the position regarding contingent, uncertain or unascertained rent consideration where, generally speaking, only one revised return will be necessary. Also, in contrast to the position with rent consideration, there is no time limit beyond which adjustments to contingent, uncertain or unascertained non-rent consideration are disregarded.

Reverse consideration

3.35 Where a freehold interest is sold, and the vendor pays the purchaser a premium for it to take the transfer, no charge to SDLT will arise on the reverse payment as the purchaser will not have given consideration for the transaction.[24] This may be common in the context of property subject to leases on unfavourable terms.

What rate of SDLT applies?

3.36 The SDLT regime in most aspects preserves the existing bands and rates of tax under stamp duty on land and property and other assets. A crucial change, however, is that the threshold in relation to commercial property has been lifted from £60,000 to £150,000. The rates[25] are listed in **tables 3A** and **3B** and operate on the same 'slab' basis as stamp duty.

---

23 S 80(2).
24 Sch 3, para 1.
25 S 55(2).

Table 3A	
Residential	
Relevant consideration	**Percentage**
Not more than £60,000	0%
More than £60,000 but not more than £250,000	1%
More than £250,000 but not more than £500,000	3%
More than £500,000	4%

Table 3B	
Commercial or mixed	
Relevant consideration	**Percentage**
Not more than £150,000	0%
More than £150,000 but not more than £250,000	1%
More than £250,000 but not more than £500,000	3%
More than £500,000	4%

The relevant consideration for the purposes of the rates above is all the consideration under the land transaction and any linked transactions. These rates do not apply to so much of the consideration for a land transaction which is rent.[26] This is taken into account under a separate regime of duty for the grant of a lease.

How do I account for SDLT?

Land transaction return – sale of freehold

3.37 Letter F should be inserted in Box 2 of the land transaction return indicating that the transaction is a transfer of a freehold interest. Depending on the nature of the freehold interest, the relevant code should be placed in Box 3. For example, for a transfer of a freehold with vacant possession, code FP should be inserted in Box 3.

---

26 S 55(6).

Where the freehold is subject to a long lease, code FG should be inserted and where the freehold is subject to an occupational lease code FT should be inserted. For these purposes, a long lease will generally be taken to be a lease granted for a premium with a ground rent rather than a market rent. At the time of writing it would appear that the Inland Revenue will require Boxes 16-22 to be completed[27] with details of any leases to which the interest being transferred is subject, but no SDLT4 need be completed in relation to these leases. Refer to the **Appendix** for complete details of how to fill in the land transaction return.

Is any ongoing compliance necessary?

3.38 It is important to recognise that further tasks may be necessary such as the filing of revised land transaction returns in the case of contingent, uncertain and unascertained consideration. It is also necessary to keep certain records should the Inland Revenue wish to commence an enquiry into the transaction, generally speaking those supporting the manner in which the return was completed (see further **para 15.26**).

Sale of freehold – examples

3.39 Sale of freehold residential property:

Mr A contracts to sell his freehold semi-detached house to Mr and Mrs B. Contracts are exchanged, at which time a deposit of 10% of the purchase price is paid to Mr A. No liability to SDLT arises at this point nor any obligation to file a land transaction return, as this does not constitute a substantial amount of the purchase price. The effective date of

---

27 Unless permission is obtained from the Inland Revenue to do otherwise (see **Appendix**, Box 23).

the transaction arises three months later when Mr and Mrs B provide the remainder of the purchase price and receive a transfer. Mr and Mrs B will be liable to pay the SDLT and file a land transaction return within 30 days of that date.

3.40 Let warehouse site:

A Ltd exchanges contracts with B Ltd on 1 December 2003 in relation to a freehold title to a vacant warehouse and some surrounding land. The warehouse is to be occupied by an electronics retailer paying quarterly rent to A Ltd. A deposit of 10% is paid. At this point no liability to SDLT arises. Two months later, and before formal completion, B Ltd requests an office decoration company to begin works necessary as part of the landlord's works. The decoration company does not vacate the property until after completion and the tenant has commenced trading from the property. Even though no document of transfer is executed by A Ltd when the construction company begins work, and B Ltd has paid nothing to A Ltd beyond the deposit, the sale of the freehold site will be regarded as substantially performed and B Ltd must lodge a land transaction return with SDLT at the applicable rates within 30 days of the decoration company commencing the fit-out works. A further land transaction return will be due on completion of the freehold transfer but no further SDLT will need to be paid at that time.

Additional issues

Exchanges of land

3.41 As with the previous stamp duty regime, it is not possible to avoid tax altogether by structuring a sale of properties as an exchange where no monetary consideration changes hands. However, whereas in certain circumstances under stamp duty it was possible to structure transactions so that only a single charge to stamp duty arose, in the context of SDLT, unless the specific exemption applies for part-exchanges of residential property (see **paras 9.82-9.85**), the exchange is treated as two separate and distinct taxable transactions.

3.42 An exchange[28] is defined as where a land transaction is entered into by a purchaser wholly or partly in consideration of another land transaction being entered into by it as vendor. The legislation further clarifies[29] that an exchange occurs in any case where an obligation to give consideration for a land transaction that a person enters into as purchaser is met wholly or partly by way of that person entering into another transaction as vendor. This clarification means that even where a contract provides for cash consideration which may be satisfied by the transfer of another property, this will be treated as an exchange for SDLT purposes, in contrast to the position under the old stamp duty 'single sale' guidance.[30] Also, the wide definition of 'exchange' precludes arrangements for the mutual sale of properties in such a way that each can be viewed as a separate sale for nominal consideration.

3.43 Where a land transaction is entered into as an exchange, the legislation[31] sets out the basis of calculation of the chargeable consideration. The basic position is that SDLT is not calculated by reference to the actual consideration but each purchaser of a chargeable interest must pay SDLT calculated on the market value of the chargeable interest it has acquired.[32] Where there are two properties involved, a more expensive property and a less expensive property, the purchaser of the less expensive property will pay SDLT by reference to the market value of the less expensive property, and the purchaser of the more expensive property

---

28 S 47(1).
29 S 47(2).
30 Inland Revenue Tax Bulletin, 3 August 1995 paras 9-12.
31 Sch 4, para 5.
32 NB – not the market value of the interest they have provided as vendor.

will pay SDLT by reference to the value of the more expensive property. Equalisation moneys are not taken into account.

3.44 Example of an exchange:

A Ltd and B Ltd own and occupy neighbouring freehold office accommodation. A Ltd owns the smaller accommodation and B Ltd the larger accommodation. A Ltd requires increased space whereas B Ltd, having fallen upon hard times, would prefer to move into A Ltd's existing offices as these are smaller. B Ltd enters into a contract with A Ltd to transfer its larger offices with a market value of £400,000 in consideration of A Ltd transferring its smaller offices with a market value of £320,000 plus equalisation monies of £80,000. A Ltd will be liable to SDLT at 3% of £400,000 in relation to its acquisition of B Ltd's offices and B Ltd will be liable to SDLT at 3% of £320,000. B Ltd thus pays SDLT at the lower amount and receives equalisation moneys which are not subject to SDLT.

3.45 Special rules apply to disregard exchanges where the only land interest involved is not a major interest in land, ie interests in land that are not freehold or leasehold interests.[33]

3.46 Where two or more properties are transferred in exchange for one, the consideration attributable to each must be calculated according to the formula set out in the legislation.[34]

3.47 Where an exchange takes place, the address of the property transferred by the purchaser in exchange needs to be inserted in Box 7. The value of the land

---

33 Finance Act 2003, s 117.
34 Sch 4, para 5(5).

acquired will be entered, or form part of the sum to be entered in Box 10 of the land transaction return. The code 37 will need to be inserted in Box 12. Box 13 should receive a 'no' response as, while there will have been an exchange, the transactions are not 'linked' in the relevant sense.

Obligations on transfer of let property

3.48 As discussed in **para 7.19**, the assumption by a purchaser of obligations in relation to leases to which a freehold interest is subject may give rise to extra chargeable consideration.[35] Thus in the case of, for example, an indemnity of the purchaser in relation to positive covenants in a lease to which the interest is subject may, in occasional circumstances, constitute extra consideration for the sale. However, it is rare in practice that such obligations will have any value.

Transactions involving a connected company

3.49 The SDLT provisions carry over the measures, introduced in the Finance Act 2000, which limit the opportunities for using connected special purpose vehicles for planning. The provisions impose a market value basis of charge where a vendor transfers or grants a lease of a property to a connected company.[36] The charge also applies where some or all of the consideration for the transaction consists of the issue or transfer of shares in a company with which the vendor is connected.

3.50 This prevents avoidance in the form of enveloping transactions, where a property is transferred to a company on a nil or low SDLT basis and the shares

---

35 Sch 17A, para 10. As not covered by exemptions in that paragraph.
36 S 53(1).

in the company are sold bearing a 0.5% stamp duty charge. This is sometimes achieved by a transfer relying on group relief, but the tightening of the requirements for this relief in recent years has discouraged this, and instead transactions have been structured to use companies owned by (eg) the families of directors that are not within the group. This provision makes the use of such companies ineffective, as an arm's length price is imposed for stamp duty/SDLT purposes.

3.51 A person is connected with a company if they have control of it or if they and persons connected with them (eg a wife, husband or relative) together have control of it.[37]

3.52 A company will be regarded as connected with another company if:

1. the same person has control of both, or a person has control of one and persons connected with them, or they and persons connected with them, have control of the other; or
2. if a group of two or more persons has control of each company, and the groups either consist of the same persons or could be regarded as consisting of the same persons by treating (in one or more cases) a member of either group as replaced by a person with whom they are connected.

3.53 A person is taken to have control of a company if that person exercises, or is able to exercise or is entitled to acquire, direct or indirect control over the company's affairs, and in particular, if such person possesses or is entitled to acquire:[38]

---

37 Income and Corporation Taxes Act 1988, s 839.
38 *Ibid*, s 416. Where two or more persons together satisfy any of the conditions they are taken to have control of the company.

1. the greater part of the share capital or issued share capital of the company or of the voting power in the company; or

2. such part of the issued share capital of the company as would, if the whole of the income of the company was in fact distributed among the participators[39] (without regard to any rights which they or any other person have as a loan creditor), entitle such person to receive the greater part of the amount so distributed; or

3. such rights as would, in the event of the winding up of the company or in any other circumstances, entitle such person to receive the greater part of the assets of the company which would then be available for distribution among the participators.

3.54 There are, however, some exceptions to the market value charge:[40]

1. Immediately after the transaction the company holds the property as trustee in the course of a business carried on by it that consists of or includes the management of trusts (this is effectively an exception for transfers to corporate trustees).

2. Immediately after the transaction the company holds the property as trustee and the vendor is connected with the company. This in broad terms covers transactions where the vendor is a settlor of a settlement and for these purposes 'connected' means a settlor, any person connected with the settlor and any company which is connected with the settlement.

3. The vendor is a company and the transaction is (or is part of) a distribution of the assets of that company (whether or not in connection with its winding up)

---

39 Broadly speaking a 'participator' is a person who has or is entitled to acquire share capital or voting rights in the company, a loan creditor, a person who has or is entitled to acquire a right to distribution or premiums payable to loan creditors or any person who is entitled to secure that income or assets of the company will be applied for their benefit.
40 S 54.

and it is not the case that the subject matter of the transaction, or an interest from which that interest is derived has, within the period of three years immediately preceding the effective date of the transaction, been the subject of a transaction in respect of which group relief was claimed by the vendor.

3.55 In addition, the transfer of the legal title only of a property to a bare trustee or nominee company would seem to be excluded from the market value charge. Transactions with a bare trustee are deemed to be the acts of the beneficial owner and thus the transaction is effectively ignored.[41]

3.56 The exercise by the trustees of a settlement of their discretion or a power of appointment will give rise to a charge to SDLT if consideration was paid for the beneficiary to become an object of the discretion or power.[42] See **para 7.23** for further details.

3.57 Example – transfers to connected companies:

Mr A owns a property and wishes to sell the property to Mr B without significant SDLT arising on the transaction. He transfers the property to a company owned by his wife for £1, and Mr B buys the company for a price reflecting the value of the property. The company will be liable to SDLT charged at the relevant rate on the full market value of the property. However, had Mr A declared the company a trustee of a settlement to be comprised of the property and transferred the property to the company for £1, this transaction would not be subject to the market value charge. Similarly, if Mr A transferred the property to a company which is a bare trustee or nominee for him, the market value charge would not arise. However, it would prove difficult for Mr A to divest himself of the equitable interest in the property and for

---

41 Sch 16, para 3.
42 Sch 16, para 7.

Mr B to acquire this interest without an SDLT charge arising at full rates as a transfer of the equitable interest would be a chargeable land transaction.

Options

3.58 The grant of an option will be liable to SDLT separately from any SDLT that arises on exercise.[43] Thus, if on 1 December 2003 A pays £100,000 for an option to purchase a property at the price of £2m, A will pay SDLT on £100,000 on the December transaction and pay SDLT again on the £2m sum when the option is exercised and the land is purchased. It is necessary to report in Box 8 of the land transaction return if a transaction is pursuant to a previous option agreement. The grant and exercise (or transactions resulting from the exercise of an option) may be treated as linked transactions. In general, there is little doubt that the option grant and exercise would be linked, which would be relevant in particular for the purposes of application of the exempt threshold.

---

43 S 46(1).

4. SALE OF A LEASEHOLD INTEREST

4.01 The sale of a leasehold interest generally raises identical issues to the sale of a freehold interest. There are however several issues that arise in the case of leasehold property transactions, which, while not exclusive to such transactions, are worth considering here.

Sale of leasehold – checklist

(a) At what point do I need to consider SDLT (see **para 4.02**)?

(b) Is the property in a disadvantaged area (see **para 4.03**)?

(c) Does any other relief apply (see **para 4.04**)?

(d) Is there any other planning I can do (see **para 4.05**)?

(e) What is the chargeable consideration (see **para 4.06**)?

    (i)   Do I take into account VAT (see **para 4.06**)?
    (ii)   Is there any non-monetary consideration (see **para 4.07**)?
    (iii) Is the consideration contingent, uncertain or unascertained (see **para 4.08**)?

(f) What rate of SDLT applies (see **para 4.15**)?

(g) How do I account for SDLT (see **para 4.16**)?

(h) Is any ongoing compliance necessary (see **para 4.18**)?

At what point do I need to consider SDLT?

4.02 The same principles will apply as regards the effective date in relation to the sale of a freehold interest. A few key points are mentioned here. In the case of a sale of a leasehold interest, the payment of 90% or more of any assignment premium will give rise to substantial performance of the assignment.[1] An early payment of rent by the assignee to the landlord will not trigger substantial

---

performance, as rent is not part of the consideration for the land transaction in question. However, if the assignee gains an early entitlement to rents under any sublease, this could indicate early possession and hence substantial performance. If the assignee or a builder on its behalf goes into occupation before completion of the assignment, this will also give rise to substantial performance of the contract. Refer to **Chapter 3** for a more detailed discussion of substantial performance.

Is the property in a disadvantaged area?

4.03 It is essential to consider whether the transaction relates to land within a disadvantaged area. Refer to **Chapter 9**.

Does any other relief apply?

4.04 Consider all the reliefs that apply in the context of freehold transfers. Refer to **Chapter 9**.

Is there any other planning I can do?

4.05 Similar techniques apply in relation to assignments of leases as transfers of freeholds. Refer to **Chapter 13**.

What is the chargeable consideration?

Do I take into account VAT?

4.06 As with the sale of a freehold interest, VAT must be taken into account as part of the chargeable consideration if it is actually charged.[2] (See **para 3.22** above for further details.) The amount of VAT should be inserted in Box 11 of the land transaction return and included in the total chargeable consideration for the purposes of Box 10. However, any VAT that is payable as a result of an option to tax exercised after completion is ignored in the calculation of chargeable consideration.

Is there any non-monetary consideration?

Obligations on assignment

4.07 As discussed in **para 7.19**, certain obligations on the assignment of a leasehold interest subject to a lease or leases in relation to the lease or leases can give rise to additional chargeable consideration to the extent (which may be rare) that these obligations have any value. However, the undertaking by the assignee of obligations under its lease would appear not to give rise to any charge.[3]

Is the consideration contingent, uncertain or unascertained?

4.08 The treatment of contingent, uncertain or unascertained consideration in the case of the sale of a leasehold interest is the same as applies to the sale of a freehold interest (see **paras 3.24-3.34**). As with the sale of a freehold interest, if there is more than one event by which uncertain consideration is made certain, there will need to be a reassessment of the taxable consideration on each of these events, and following each of these events a revised land transaction return may be due within 30 days. Also, in the case of contingent and uncertain (but not unascertained) consideration, payment of SDLT may be deferred (see **para 14.99**).

---

2 Sch 4, para 2.
3 Sch 17A, para 17.

4.09 Where a lease granted for contingent, uncertain or unascertained consideration (note that a rent review within five years of the date of grant makes the consideration uncertain) is assigned, the legislation[4] clarifies that it is the assignee of the lease that bears responsibility for submitting any further returns with the extra SDLT payable.

Reverse consideration

4.10 Where a leasehold interest is sold, and the outgoing tenant pays the incoming tenant a premium for him to take the lease, no charge to SDLT will arise.[5]

Anti-avoidance measures

4.11 In order to counter avoidance on the grant of leases by the assignment (for no taxable consideration) of leases that have already had the benefit of certain exemptions on grant, the assignment is deemed to be the grant of a new lease. This is in effect a clawback of the exemption. The exemptions that are subject to this measure are as follows:[6]

1. sale and leaseback provisions (see **para 6.07** below);
2. group relief, reconstruction or acquisition relief (see **paras 9.34-9.60** below);
3. transfers involving public bodies (see **para 9.121** below);
4. charities relief (see **para 9.61-9.67** below); and
5. exemptions under certain regulations.[7]

---

4 Sch 17A, para 12.
5 Sch 4, para 15(1).
6 Sch 17A, para 11.
7. Regulations made pursuant to s 123(3), ie regulations reproducing for SDLT certain exemptions that applied to stamp duty.

Where a lease which benefitted from one of the above reliefs is assigned, the new lease is deemed to be granted on identical terms to the actual lease and for a term equal to the unexpired term of the actual lease.

4.12 The effect of these provisions is to prevent company A granting a lease to its subsidiary, company B, and then company B, having claimed group relief, assigning that lease to a third party, effectively the intended tenant. In this situation, the intra-group lease would become chargeable on assignment by virtue of the deeming of a grant of a lease by company B to the third-party tenant.

4.13 In light of the anti-avoidance provisions, in the context of an assignment transaction, the purchaser should raise an enquiry as to whether any relevant reliefs have been claimed. In certain circumstances, for example in asset sale transactions a warranty and/or indemnity in this respect may be advisable.

4.14 Example:

---

*Company X transfers land to company Y in return for a 35 year lease for a rent of £100,000 per annum. As a result of the sale and leaseback provisions (see **para 6.07**) SDLT is only payable by reference to the market value of the land transferred and not also on the lease. However, if company X then assigns the lease to company Z, that assignment will be treated as the grant of a new lease and SDLT will need to be paid on the NPV of the unexpired term of the lease.*

What rate of SDLT applies?

4.15 The same rates of tax apply as in relation to transfers of freehold interests (refer to **para 3.36**).

How do I account for SDLT?

Land transaction return

4.16 As the transaction is a transfer, code F should be inserted in Box 2. Depending on the nature of the leasehold interest a different code will need to be inserted in Box 3. Where a leasehold interest is a long lease transferred with vacant possession, code LG should be inserted in Box 3. Where the leasehold interest is a long lease subject to an occupational lease, the relevant code is LT. In the case of the assignment of an occupational lease, the relevant code is LP. In all other cases of leasehold assignments the code is OT. For these purposes, a long lease will generally be taken to be a lease granted for a premium with a ground rent rather than a market rent.

4.17 Unless you receive permission otherwise,[8] Boxes 16-22 will need to be completed with details of any leases to which the assignment is subject, but no SDLT4 need be completed. Nor is it necessary to complete Boxes 16-22 with details of the lease being assigned. It would appear that details of the lease itself which is being assigned need not be entered in these boxes.

Is any ongoing compliance necessary?

4.18 Particular ongoing compliance issues arise in the context of assignments of leases granted for contingent, uncertain or unascertained consideration. If the rent becomes certain, it will be the assignee's responsibility to file a revised land transaction return. However, as explained in **Chapter 5**, after the end of the fifth year

---

8 See **Appendix**.

of the lease the liability to file a revised land transaction return ceases provided there is no 'abnormal' increase in rent. In addition to these issues, the assignee will need to keep certain records, broadly those supporting the manner in which the return was completed.

5. THE GRANT OF A LEASE

5.01 As with the outgoing stamp duty regime, the SDLT regime imposes a separate charge on the grant of a lease from the charge on the transfer of a freehold or leasehold interest. Thus an entirely different basis of calculation of tax applies to so much of the consideration for a land transaction as consists of rent. The same regime as that applying to transfers applies to any premium consideration given for the grant of a lease. Unlike most sale transactions, the grant of a lease will more commonly involve ongoing compliance issues following the transaction, as discussed at the end of this chapter.

5.02 The charge to SDLT on rent applies in respect of all chargeable transactions for which the chargeable consideration consists of or includes rent, or where such consideration falls to be taken into account as a linked transaction.[1]

5.03 Thus the charge to SDLT on rent will apply not only on the grant of a lease in respect of the rent consideration, but also on other transactions relating to a chargeable land interest where the consideration has the nature of rent. The SDLT regime does not define 'rent'. Rather, the term 'rent' is a term which has its meaning in land law. The distinction is outlined further below in **para 5.27**.

Definition of lease

5.04 Schedule 17A provides that a 'lease' means an interest or right in or over land for a term of years (whether fixed or periodic) or a tenancy at will or other

---

1 Sch 5, para 1.

interest or right in or over land terminable by notice at any time.[2] The authors understand that tenancies at will are exempt[3] and will not be treated as subject to SDLT notwithstanding that they have been specifically included within the definition of 'lease' by the Variation Regulations.[4]

5.05 Periodic payments under a licence are not subject to SDLT as licences to use or occupy land are excluded from the category of chargeable interests.[5] Similarly, advowsons, franchises and manorial rights are excluded.[6]

5.06 It is therefore important to determine the distinction between a lease and a licence. Generally speaking, and as decided by *Street v Mountford*[7] and cases which have followed it, the key difference between a lease and a licence is that a lease gives the tenant exclusive possession. A licence merely allows the licensee on to the premises without being regarded as a trespasser, but the licensor can still remain on the premises. Thus where, for example, a trader is given the right to trade in a cinema and is allowed to set up its stall wherever permitted by the occupier at the time, the trader will have a licence, but as it has no exclusive possession of any particular area of the premises, it will not have a lease. Similarly, if the landlord can direct that an occupier uses different parts of the premises in exchange with other occupiers or can only come on to the premises at particular times in the week, this would be indicative of a licence. In some circumstances, the question may be whether the right is a licence or another right, such as a right of way over land, and in these circumstances it should be noted that while a genuine licence is not subject to SDLT, a right of way is a chargeable interest.

---

2 Sch 17A, para 1.
3 S 48(2).
4 Sch 17A, para 1.
5 S 48(2)(b).
6 S 48(2)(c).
7 [1985] AC 809.

5.07 While a licence is an exempt interest, occupation pursuant to a licence where such occupation leads to the substantial performance of an agreement for lease will result in the payment under the licence being treated as payment under the substantially performed agreement for lease, and thus falling into charge.

Grant of a lease – checklist

(a) At what point do I need to consider SDLT (see **para 5.08**)?

(b) Is the property in a disadvantaged area (see **para 5.23**)?

(c) Does any other relief apply (see **para 5.24**)?

(d) Is there any other planning I can do (see **para 5.25**)?

(e) What is the chargeable consideration (see **para 5.26**)?

    (i)   Do I take into account VAT (see **para 5.29**)?
    (ii)   Is there any non-monetary consideration (see **para 5.31**)?
    (iii)   Is the consideration contingent, uncertain or unascertained (see **para 5.32**)?

(f) How do I calculate lease duty (see **para 5.57**)?

(g) How do I account for SDLT on a lease (see **para 5.78**)?

(h) Is any ongoing compliance necessary (see **para 5.80**)?

At what point do I need to consider SDLT?

5.08 When does the charge to SDLT arise? This depends on the 'effective date of the transaction'. The basic rule is that the effective date is the completion of the transaction,[8] but this may be earlier if, broadly speaking, the price is paid earlier or the tenant goes into occupation earlier.[9] The effective date must be inserted in Box 4 of the land transaction return. The effective date of a transaction is the material date for liability to arise, and from which 30 days are given

---

8 S 44(3).
9 S 44(4).

for a land transaction return to be lodged at the Inland Revenue together with the tax.[10]

5.09 An agreement for lease does not give rise to a charge to SDLT until it is completed, which is the effective date. When a transaction is completed, the charge to SDLT arises and the agreement and the transaction on completion are treated as a single land transaction.[11] However, if the agreement for lease has already been substantially performed before completion, then a charge to SDLT will arise by reference to the date of substantial performance of the agreement.[12] There will be a further land transaction when a lease is granted pursuant to a substantially performed agreement for lease as explained in **para 5.21** below.

5.10 An agreement for lease is substantially performed where either:

1. a substantial amount of the consideration is paid or provided[13] (likely to be more relevant in the case of a lease granted for a premium) ('early consideration'); or

2. the purchaser or a person connected with the purchaser takes possession of the whole, or substantially the whole of the subject matter of the contract ('early possession').

Early consideration

5.11 In the context of an agreement for lease, consideration will be paid early when:

---

10 Ss 76(1) and 86(1).
11 S 44(3).
12 S 44(4).
13 S 44(5).

1. 90% or more of the premium is paid or provided; or

2. a payment of rent is made.

5.12 The SDLT Manual[14] clarifies that 'a substantial amount of the consideration' will be 90% or more of the total consideration payable. Therefore, if at the time an agreement for grant of a long lease for a premium is entered into, a deposit of 10% of the consideration is paid, this will not constitute substantial performance of the agreement for lease, and thus will not yet give rise to a liability to SDLT. The SDLT Manual further clarifies that the 90% rule will not apply where the circumstances of the transaction are such that (in substance) the whole of the consideration has in fact been provided. It gives the example of a contract providing for the purchase of a property with a market value of £10m for a total consideration of £15m, £10m payable in 2004 and the remainder in 2099. In these circumstances the transaction will be regarded as already having been substantially performed.

5.13 If a deposit of 90% or more of the consideration is paid and held on an agency basis, it is the authors' view that this would most likely constitute substantial performance. If such a deposit was paid and held on a stakeholder basis, in the authors' view the position is less clear. The vendor would not be entitled to access the deposit moneys and therefore the purchaser may not be considered to have paid or provided the consideration. However, even in this scenario it seems arguable that the consideration has been provided by the purchaser.

5.14 As a result of the substantial performance condition, it will not be possible to avoid a charge to SDLT by the parties entering into an agreement for

---

14 Para 7950.

grant of (eg) a long lease and the tenant paying the premium without taking a grant ('resting on contract'). Under SDLT, as soon as a substantial amount of the premium is paid, the transaction becomes liable to SDLT.

5.15 Where the only consideration is rent, substantial performance will occur when the first payment of rent is made if this is before completion.[15] If the consideration for a land transaction consists of both rent and other consideration, substantial performance will occur on the earlier of either the occasion when 90% of the non-rent consideration is paid or when the first payment of rent is made.[16]

Early possession

5.16 In the context of an agreement for lease, possession will be taken early when a person takes physical possession of the land.

5.17 The taking of physical possession will constitute substantial performance, such as where the tenant goes into occupation or moves eg plant or equipment on to the site. It is immaterial whether the possession is taken under the agreement itself or under a licence or lease of a temporary character.[17] It should be noted that while a licence is an exempt interest, an agreement for lease can be substantially performed by possession pursuant to a licence, with the result that the periodic payments under the licence become chargeable to SDLT. This means that in the common situation where a tenant, or, eg a building company at the tenant's order, enters the site early under a licence in order to carry out works, substantial

---

15 S 44(7)(b).
16 S 44(7)(c).
17 S 44(6).

performance will already have taken place. It is thought that wherever a builder is commissioned by the tenant, the same conclusion would apply even if the works are solely for the benefit of the landlord. The SDLT Manual[18] states that the commencement of fitting-out works will constitute the taking of possession, and thus substantial performance if the trade commences once the fitting-out works are completed. This does not, it would appear, mean that substantial performance is deemed not to have occurred if there is a hiatus between the time the works are completed and the tenant's trade commences. However, if the landlord takes back occupation of the land after the building works, this would show that the landlord is still in control of the land and that the tenant had not yet taken possession.

5.18 A further issue is what happens where the tenant goes into physical possession but only occupies a small part of the building. In these circumstances it might be said that the tenant had not taken possession of 'substantially the whole' of the subject matter of the agreement for lease. The authors understand that the question of substantial performance requires an examination of the factual background. Thus, if the landlord still owns and bears the risk of the remainder of the land, the tenant may not have taken possession. For example, if the landlord still provides a fence and security for the land during the course of construction, this may indicate that even though the tenant is occupying part, the land is still effectively controlled by the landlord. If it is only due to a lack of resources that the builder is solely carrying out works to part of the land, this may show that the tenant has in fact taken possession. The 90% guideline as regards the meaning of 'substantially the whole' may also be used in this context, but it should be emphasised that this is not a hard and fast rule.

---

18 Para 7900a.

5.19 Sometimes a superior lease is granted subject to existing leases (an 'overriding lease'). In the circumstances of such a lease, the early receipt of rents by the intended overriding tenant may also give rise to substantial performance by virtue of early possession.

5.20 In order for there to be substantial performance, there needs to be an agreement which can be substantially performed. Where there is no agreement for lease and a tenant has been allowed into possession before the lease is signed, the lease will not have been substantially performed, but some other interest such as a licence or tenancy at will may have been granted.

Completion after substantial performance

5.21 Where an agreement for lease has been substantially performed, giving rise to an effective date prior to completion, this will not be the end of the matter. The substantial performance of an agreement for lease is a notifiable land transaction. The completion of an agreement for lease by the grant of a lease will constitute a further notifiable land transaction,[19] and SDLT will need to be paid on that second land transaction to the extent that the tax payable exceeds that payable on the earlier land transaction. Even if the consideration payable on completion is identical to the contractual consideration, two land transaction returns will need to be submitted, one within 30 days of substantial performance of the agreement for lease and another within 30 days of completion.[20] The Inland Revenue has instituted a special procedure whereby the second land transaction return is submitted to the Manchester Stamp Office, which intervenes to prevent SDLT being charged twice. See **para 14.55** for more details.

---

19 S 44(8).
20 SDLT Manual, para 00890.

5.22 Where an agreement for lease has been substantially performed but is later rescinded, annulled or otherwise not carried into effect, any tax paid by virtue of substantial performance can be reclaimed from the Inland Revenue by submission of an amended land transaction return. The legislation does not give the Inland Revenue discretion to refuse such a repayment of SDLT. Where the agreement for lease is only partially rescinded, annulled or otherwise not carried into effect, a partial refund will be made. Thus if an agreement for lease relating to two plots of land is substantially performed by the purchaser paying 90% or more of the purchase consideration and SDLT is paid as required, if the contract is then varied so that only one plot is subject to the sale, the tax attributable to the consideration relating to the other plot may be reclaimed.

Is the property in a disadvantaged area?

5.23 Disadvantaged area relief applies in same way to rent. In the case of rent, the £150,000 cap in relation to residential land applies to the NPV of the rents payable under the lease (see **Chapter 9**). In particular, it should be noted that if the average annual rent is in excess of £600 then if any premium is also payable, disadvantaged area relief will not apply if the land in question is residential.[21]

Does any other relief apply?

5.24 See **Chapter 9** which summarises all the reliefs and exemptions in the context of SDLT. Certain reliefs are specific to leases, such as the grant of leases to registered social landlords, sale and leaseback, and the reliefs applicable to surrenders and regrants.

---

21 Sch 6, para 5(4). This rule has no bearing on land which is wholly commercial.

Is there any other planning I can do?

5.25 See **Chapter 13** which discusses planning generally. It may be worth consider-ing the grant of a licence as an alternative to a lease, but it may be difficult to ensure that the interest granted is genuinely a licence, and a licence may not be attractive to a prospective tenant. Where possible, the purchase of existing leases should be explored as a means of obtaining a lease without SDLT liability. However, it will need to be checked that the lease did not benefit from certain reliefs on grant which could be clawed back at the expense of the purchaser of the lease. You may also wish to make use of short leases with options to renew. It should be borne in mind that these will generally not achieve a saving of SDLT, only a deferral, and that the rates of SDLT may have increased by the time the option to renew is exercised. As each of the leases granted pursuant to the option to renew will be treated as linked with the first lease, a land transaction return will need to be submitted on the grant of the second and later leases in the series, accounting for SDLT on the basis of the NPV of the aggregate term less the SDLT already accounted for.[23]

What is the chargeable consideration?

5.26 Any premium and rent paid in consideration for the grant of the lease will constitute chargeable consideration. Some leases are granted for a premium and no rent, some for rent and no premium and some for both rent and premium but generally most leases are in two forms, either granted at a substantial rent for a period of 25 years or less, or granted for a substantial premium, a significant term and a ground rent, rather than a market rent. Any consideration which is not rent is premium consideration.

---

23 Sch 17A, para 5(1).

5.27 Rent generally means a payment reserved by the lessor on the demise of land – *IRC v Hatherton*.[24] It has also been described as the total monetary payment under an instrument of letting – *Mackworth v Hellard*.[25] Sums paid to a landlord in respect of rates and services charges will fall to be included.[26] A leading textbook states that the key features of rent are that it is: i) a periodical sum; ii) paid in return for occupation of land which; iii) issues out of the land; and iv) for non-payment of which a distress is leviable.[27]

5.28 Service charge and insurance premiums payable under a lease are often reserved as rent to ensure that the remedy of distress is available in respect of non-payment of these amounts. Where this is the case, doubt remains as to whether these payments are included within the rent consideration, but the authors believe that, pending Inland Revenue guidance, the better view is that provided the apportionment to these items is genuine, the amounts payable are not brought into account as chargeable consideration.

Do I take into account VAT?

5.29 Any VAT actually charged as a result of the exercise of the option to tax is taken into account as part of the chargeable rent. However, if the option to tax is exercised after the effective date of the transaction, this will be disregarded and will not constitute additional contingent consideration.[28]

5.30 Example:

---

24 [1936] 2 KB 316
25 [1921] 2 KB 755
26 *Halsbury's Laws of England* – Landlord and Tenant – 15, para 708.

27 *Woodfall's Law of Landlord and Tenant* (Looseleaf ed, Sweet & Maxwell, Release 56), para 7001.
28 Sch 4, para 2.

An agreement for lease is substantially performed by the prospective tenant entering the premises early to commence fitting-out works. This will constitute the effective date of the transaction. Some weeks later, just before the lease is granted pursuant to the agreement for lease, the landlord exercises the option to charge VAT on the rents. SDLT will need to be paid to the Inland Revenue within 30 days of the effective date of the land transaction constituted by the substantial performance of the agreement for lease, and should not include VAT in the calculation. However, when the lease is granted, this will be regarded as a further notifiable land transaction and the option to charge VAT will have been made before the effective date of this transaction. Accordingly, the land transaction return due at that date should report the further chargeable consideration due in the form of VAT.

Is there any non-monetary consideration?

5.31 The legislation includes a wide definition of chargeable consideration, which can include many categories of non-monetary consideration. Non-monetary consideration is more common in relation to premiums, but may be encountered occasionally in the context of rent. Any consideration in money or money's worth will constitute chargeable consideration. See **Chapter 7** which explains the treatment of non-monetary consideration.

Is the consideration contingent, uncertain or unascertained?

Contingent, uncertain or unascertained premium consideration

5.32 As regards contingent, uncertain or unascertained consideration for the grant of a lease which does not consist of rent, the treatment is the same in relation to the sale of freehold and leasehold interests. See **Chapter 3** above.

Contingent, uncertain or unascertained consideration consisting of rent

5.33 Refer to **Chapter 2** which explains the difference between contingent, uncertain and unascertained consideration. Generally speaking, contingent rent consideration will arise where a lease specifies that the rent will go up or down by a particular amount if a certain event does or does not occur. Uncertain rent is where the rent in the lease may vary according to future events and there is no pre-determined amount that would be payable according to those future events. This includes rents that vary in accordance with turnover, rents which vary according to rental receipts under other leases (eg shared rent leases) and, importantly, rents that vary according to a rent review provision in the lease. Unascertained rent is where the rent at the effective date has not yet been fixed, but depends on events on or prior to the effective date rather than on future events.

Basis of assessment of contingent, uncertain or unascertained rent

5.34 *Contingent rent* – when a lease is granted for contingent rent, a land transaction return must be lodged within 30 days of the effective date of the transaction, with SDLT calculated on the rents on the assumption that the outcome of the contingency is that the extra rent is payable, or, as the case may be, that the maximum amount of the rent does not cease to be payable.[29]

5.35 *Uncertain or unascertained rent* – when a lease is granted for uncertain or unascertained rent, a land transaction return must be lodged within 30 days of the effective date of the transaction. The return must include a reasonable estimate of

---

29 S 51(1).

the NPV of the lease upon which SDLT is calculated. In many cases, this will require a forecast of future events. This is necessary, for example, in relation to turnover leases where the turnover of occupying businesses need to be forecast, or in the case of geared rental leases where rental receipts of the occupational leases need to be estimated. The Inland Revenue does not seem to require a market valuation provided by independent experts. A good estimate should be sufficient, in the knowledge that if the estimate is an underestimate, further SDLT will be payable at a later date.[30]

5.36 If the rent ceases to be contingent, uncertain or unascertained ('uncertain') before the end of the fifth year of the term of the lease, a revised land transaction return should be submitted if the circumstances listed in **para 5.38** below apply within 30 days of the date of the rent becoming certain with any SDLT or extra SDLT due.[31] For these purposes, the 'term' is the term of the lease measured in accordance with the rules discussed in **para 5.70** below. If, at the end of the fifth year of the term the rent remains uncertain, a revised land transaction return should be submitted within 30 days of that date, accounting for SDLT based on the rent paid during the first five years of the term.[32] For the purpose of calculating lease duty on grant, any event after the end of the fifth year of the term is disregarded and the rent which is taken into account for the remainder of the term is the highest rent payable during any period of 12 consecutive months in the first five years of the term.

5.37 To summarise the basic principle as regards adjustments up to and including the end of the first five years of the lease, a reassessment of the chargeable rent consideration is required in that period on whichever is the earlier of:

---

30 S 51(2).
31 Sch 17A, para 8(1).
32 Sch 17A, para 8(3).

1. the date upon which the rent payable for the whole of the first five years of the lease is known; and

2. the end of the first five years of the term.

5.38 A revised return will need to be submitted in respect of the first five years of the term of the lease if either:[33]

1. a transaction that was not previously notifiable becomes notifiable;

2. additional tax is payable; or

3. tax is payable where none was previously payable.

5.39 The tax paid when the revised return is submitted should be calculated on the basis of rates in force at the effective date of the transaction. If less tax is payable, an application may be made to reclaim the excess tax paid.[34] Where the term of a lease is less than five years, the Inland Revenue suggests that termination will be deemed the end of the fifth year of the lease for the purposes of reconsidering any contingent, uncertain or unascertained rent.

5.40 The principles above apply generally to rent which is contingent, uncertain or unascertained. It is worth looking at how these principles apply in the context of:

1. rent reviews (most commonly upward-only rent reviews provided for in the lease);

2. stepped rent increases (there are specified increases in rent contained in the lease which are ascertained at the date of grant); and

---

33 Sch 17A, para 8(3).
34 Sch 17A, para 8(5).

3.   equity rents (which include turnover leases, geared rent leases and side by side leases. This category contains all cases of rents that vary according to the rent paid under other leases or by reference to performance such as the profits or turnover of a related commercial activity.)

The regulations laid following the end of the consultation on lease duty introduced a rigorous and complex regime for taking rent increases into account to replace the simpler regime first appearing in the Finance Act 2003. The aim of these provisions is to prevent the avoidance of SDLT by the grant of leases at reduced rent where there is some means of increasing the rent to market rates after grant. The provisions bring the rules for increases within the regime for contingent, uncertain and unascertained consideration. The basic aim of these rules is to prevent the need for repeated reassessment of the rent consideration, but as may be seen, in some cases more than one further filing is required, such as where the rent is still not determined at the end of the fifth year of the term.

Rent reviews

Position until end of fifth year

5.41 An ordinary rent review is an event which makes rent cease to be uncertain for the purposes of the rules on contingent, uncertain and unascertained consideration. Thus, if a rent review takes effect before the end of the fifth year of the term, a revised land transaction return must be submitted within 30 days of that date, unless the rent payable in respect of the first five years of the term is not determined until the end of the fifth year of the term or later. Where the rent for the first five years is not determined at the end of the fifth year of the term (but the rent review takes effect before the end of the fifth year), a revised land transaction return must be submitted at the five-year point, based on the rent paid in the first five years and an amended version of the revised return will need to be submitted once the reviewed rent is known. Where the reviewed rent is known but the rent remains uncertain for other reasons (eg a turnover rent), again the revised return will be due not at the date of the rent review but at the end of the fifth year of the term.

5.42 The term of the lease for SDLT purposes is identified by reference to the rules discussed in **para 5.70**. The five-year principle can give rise to difficulties as a result of the rules for determining the end of the fifth year of the term. Depending on how the rent review provisions in a lease are drafted, what might normally be regarded as a five-yearly rent review may give rise to a first rent review before termination of the fifth year of the lease for the purposes of the rent increase provisions. For example, if a lease specifies that the term commencement date is 25 December 2003, and that rent reviews are required to take effect at five-yearly intervals from term commencement but the lease is granted shortly after, eg on 1 January 2004, the end of the fifth year of the term as counted from grant will be seven days later than the fifth anniversary of term commencement, ie 25 December 2008. Thus there would be a requirement for the rent review taking effect on that date to be taken into account, however small the increase in rent and a revised land transaction return will need to be filed with the Inland Revenue. One way to prevent this situation is to ensure that the rent review anniversaries correspond with the date of grant. This solution may not always be commercially acceptable, such as where it is desired for the rent reviews in all the units in a shopping centre to coincide.

Position following end of fifth year

5.43 After the end of the fifth year, rent increases (including those pursuant to a rent review) will be disregarded unless such increases are 'abnormal'. The relevant figure of rent for any period after the end of the fifth year of the term to be inserted in the lease duty NPV formula is the highest amount of rent payable (whether constant or not) in respect of any consecutive 12-month period in the first five years of the term.[35] This figure is relevant to the NPV calculation (see **para 5.62** regarding the lease duty calculator) on grant and to the reassessment of rent consideration where the rent payable for the first five years of the term ceases to be contingent, uncertain or unascertained.

'Abnormal' increases after fifth year

5.44 An increase in rent will be treated as the grant of a new lease for a rent equivalent to the excess of the increased rent over that payable before the increase if it is regarded as 'abnormal'.[36] Where such a new lease is deemed to have been granted, the new lease is regarded as a land transaction linked with the lease granted before the abnormal increase, which may bring the consideration over the applicable exempt threshold. If there has been an 'abnormal' increase a new land transaction return will need to be lodged with SDLT payable, despite the fact that the increase takes place after the end of the fifth year of the term.

5.45 In order to determine whether an increase in rent is abnormal, it is necessary to take the 'starting rent', being the highest amount of rent payable in the first five years (or the rent as a result of the last 'abnormal' increase) as described in **para 5.43** above and, according to a series of steps set out in the legislation, determine whether the rent has risen by more than the Retail Price Index – plus the permitted uplift (broadly speaking 5% per annum).[37]

---

35 Sch 17A, para 7(3).
36 Sch 17A, para 14(2).
37 Sch 17A, para 15.

5.46 The Inland Revenue has stated that the 'abnormal increase' provisions do not apply to leases with an effective date prior to 1 December 2003. Therefore, the earliest these provisions could apply would be 1 December 2008. Accordingly, the application of these provisions need not be cause for immediate concern. Further, the Inland Revenue has indicated that it is open to consultation on alternative measures which could similarly prevent avoidance by the grant of leases at reduced rent. For this reason, the exact method of calculating an abnormal increase is not set out in this text, but may be viewed on the accompanying CD-Rom. The Inland Revenue has not produced an electronic form of calculator in relation to abnormal increases at the time of writing. Once a lease is assigned, responsibility for any subsequent abnormal increases will rest with the assignee.

5.47 Example:

A 20-year lease specifies that the rent will be £5,000 per annum until the end of the third year of the lease, after which the rent will increase to £7,000 per annum. Following the fifth year, the rent is to be reviewed every five years according to a standard rent review clause. In this example, the rent to be taken into account in relation to the first, second and third years of the lease will be £5,000. For subsequent years until expiry of the lease, the rent to be taken into account will ordinarily be £7,000 notwithstanding any further rent reviews. However, if five years later the rent doubles to £14,000 (assuming inflation remained low) this would constitute an abnormal increase and on such rent review a new lease would be deemed to be granted for the excess rent, ie £7,000, and SDLT will have to be accounted for on this basis.

5.48 Further example:

In an alternative scenario the lease, rather than specifying an amount of rent applicable at the third year, states that at the third year a rent review is triggered. In these circumstances, assuming the rent was reviewed to £7,000 this figure would then be insert-ed in the revised land transaction return that would have to be submitted within 30 days of the date from which such review takes place (unless the rent continued to be uncertain until the end of the fifth year of the lease). Then, as with the main example, £7,000 would continue to be the relevant rent for SDLT purposes for the remainder of the term notwithstanding any further reviews unless an abnormal increase resulted from a rent review.

Stepped increases

Position until end of fifth year

5.49 All increases provided for in the lease until the end of the fifth year of the term are taken into account in the original lease duty calculation that must be made for the purposes of calculating SDLT due at the effective date of the transaction.

Position after end of fifth year

5.50 Any increases provided for in the lease after the end of the fifth year of the term are ignored both for the purposes of the lease duty liability on grant and for the purposes of any later adjustments to the chargeable consideration. However, if a stated increase constitutes an abnormal increase (and this can only be known at the date of such events, due to the index-linked element in the 'abnormal increase' calculation) a revised return must be submitted with any extra SDLT due within 30 days of such increase taking effect, even though such increase occurs after the end of the fifth year of the term.

Equity rents

Position until end of fifth year

5.51 In the case of equity rents, there will usually not be a single event upon which the rents cease to be uncertain. Rather, the rents in respect of the whole term of the lease will continue to be uncertain throughout the term, even once the rent for a particular expired year of the term is set. The rules nevertheless operate so that no reassessment of the rent will be due until the end of the fifth year of the term. Within 30 days of the end of the fifth year of the term, a revised land transaction return must be submitted, based on the rents paid during the first five years of the term and assuming that the rents payable for the remainder of the term will be equivalent to the highest rent paid in any 12 consecutive months during the first five years of the term. If the rent in relation to any part of the first five years of the term is not fixed by the end of the first five years of the term, in addition to the return filed at the end of the first five years, an amended return will need to be submitted when the rent for that period is finally determined.

Position after end of fifth year

5.52 Any events after the end of the fifth year, as a result of which the rent for any period ceases to be uncertain, are ignored. Thus the finalisation of, eg turnover accounts, in relation to a period after the fifth year of the term will be disregarded. However, if, as a result of an event after the end of the fifth year of the term, the rent increases by an 'abnormal' amount (as defined above) a revised land transaction return will need to be submitted with the extra SDLT due.

5.53 Example:

A lease of a shopping centre is granted to a property investor by a local authority, specifying that the property investor must pay to the landlord, in addition to a fixed rent of £1m per annum, a percentage of the rent payable under all the shop leases. At the date of grant, lease duty must be paid on the fixed rent plus a reasonable estimate of the element derived from the shop leases. At the fifth year of the lease, a revised land transaction return must be submitted, calculated on the rent paid in the first five years of the lease. The highest rent payable during any 12 consecutive months in the first five years of the term would then be assumed to be the rent payable for the remainder of the term and would be taken into account in the NPV calculation in the revised return submitted at the end of the fifth year of the term.

5.54 Where a lease granted for contingent, uncertain or unascertained consideration is assigned, the question arises whether the assignor or the assignee is responsible for accounting for any further SDLT that becomes payable following assignment, and for lodging a revised land transaction return. The legislation[38] clarifies that it is the assignee of the lease that bears responsibility for submitting any further returns with the extra SDLT payable.

5.55 The obligation to reconsider the SDLT payable where the consideration is contingent uncertain or unascertained does not apply to annuities.[39]

5.56 In the case of right-to-buy transactions, contingent consideration does not count as chargeable consideration.[40] However, uncertain and unascertained consideration would count, but may be rare in right-to-buy scenarios.

---

38 Sch 17A, para 12.
39 S 52(7).
40 Sch 9, para 1(1).

How do I calculate lease duty?

5.57 You will need to carry out a separate SDLT calculation for any premium and any rent consideration. The calculation of premium consideration follows the principles in **Chapter 3**.

How do I calculate lease duty on rents?

5.58 The tax is calculated as a percentage of the NPV of the rent payable over the term of the lease.[41] The NPV is the total rent payable subject to a temporal discount rate currently fixed at 3.5%. Depending on whether the chargeable interest is residential or commercial, different bands apply[42] The relevant rent value will include rent under any linked transactions.

Table 5A	
Residential	
Relevant rental value	**Percentage**
Up to £60,000	0%
Excess over £60,000	1%

Table 5B	
Commercial or mixed	
Relevant rental value	**Percentage**
Up to £150,000	0%
Excess over £150,000	1%

5.59 An alternative method for calculating lease duty is to apply the relevant rate to the whole consideration and then deduct £1,500 from the resulting

---

41 Sch 5, para 2(2).
42 Sch 5, para 2(3).

figure if the land is commercial and £600 from the resulting figure if the land is residential.

5.60 Unlike SDLT on transfers and premiums a 'slice', and not a 'slab' system, applies in relation to lease duty on rents, so that the 1% rate applies to any excess NPV over the nil-rate band. The following formula applies to calculate the SDLT on rent:

$$V = \sum_{i=1}^{n} \frac{r_i}{(1+T)^i}$$

Where: r_i is the rent payable

               i is the first, second third, etc, year of the term

               n is the term of the lease

               T is the temporal discount rate

5.61 The lease duty formula works by adding up the rent payable throughout the term of the lease and applying a discount rate of 3.5% to reach the NPV of the lease. The taxable amount of the NPV is the excess of the NPV over the relevant exempt threshold. To calculate tax on this amount, the rate of 1% is applied to the resulting figure. The NPV of the lease is inserted in Box 23 of the land transaction return. Where one or more additional transactions for which the chargeable consideration consists of or includes rent falls to be treated as a linked transaction, only one exempt band is apportioned between the transactions and the formula in the legislation should be used to determine the application of the exempt band.[43]

---

43 Sch 5, para 2(6).

It is important to note that there is no refund of SDLT payable in relation to the outstanding term of the lease where a lease comes to an end, whether by virtue of the exercise of a break right, surrender, forfeiture or otherwise.

5.62 To assist with the NPV calculations the Inland Revenue has provided an electronic calculator, which is included on the CD-Rom with this book. However, it is expected that the Inland Revenue may update this calculator, and we would recommend that you check for updates on www.inlandrevenue.gov.uk/so/sdlt_index.htm. The lease duty calculator in operation at the time of writing asks:

1. Whether the property is residential, commercial or mixed. If the property is mixed, there is no apportionment and the commercial bands apply.

2. Whether the property is in a disadvantaged area. If the property is mixed (ie both residential and commercial) the calculator will not provide a correct answer if the land is also disadvantaged, unless an apportionment is first made between the land that is residential and the land which is commercial.

3. For any premium amount. The calculator performs an SDLT calculation both on the premium and the rent.

4. For the lease term – part years cannot be entered.

5. For the rent payable in each of the first five years of the lease. Only the rent payable in the first five years is required because rent increases after five years are ignored. Where a lease is granted for a term which does not correspond to a number of whole years, for the first year of the term include only the portion of rents that corresponds to the fraction of the year.

6. For 'the highest 12 monthly rent in the first five-year period'. As explained above in **para 5.43** while rent increases after the first five years of the term are ignored, the rent which is deemed to apply for SDLT

purposes for the remainder of the term is the highest rent payable in a consecutive 12-month period in the first five years of the term. This box in the calculator should only be completed if the term of the lease is in excess of five years.

7. The calculator finally asks whether the average annual rent for the lease is greater than £600. This is because, as explained below, if the average annual rent is in excess of £600 the nil-rate band does not apply to the premium and the rate of 1% applies instead.

5.63 At the time of writing, the Inland Revenue online SDLT calculator does not expressly cater for leases which are for a term which does not correspond to a whole number of years.

5.64 Further, as explained in **para 5.70** below, the term of a lease for SDLT purposes does not necessarily commence at the contractual term commencement date, as the term of the lease will be counted, eg from the date of access. As mentioned above, the Inland Revenue has however indicated that the calculator may be used by inputting the total rent actually payable during the part year in question in order to achieve the correct result.

5.65 The Inland Revenue has provided tables of multiplication factors[44] which may be used more flexibly than the electronic calculator in order to calculate lease duty. The use of the tables is explained in the accompanying notes. These tables may be found on the CD-Rom accompanying this book.

5.66 Any increases in rent by reference to the Retail Price Index or inflation are ignored in the calculation. Break clauses are also ignored.

---

44 Stamp Duty Information Bulletin Issue 6.

How do I calculate lease duty on a premium?

5.67 Where a lease is granted for a premium, the transfer basis of SDLT applies at the rates specified in **para 3.36**.

5.68 Where a lease is granted for a premium and rent, and the average annual rent exceeds £600, even if the premium for grant of the lease is sufficiently low to fit within the relevant 0% band (ie £60,000 or less for residential, £150,000 or less for commercial) the 1% rate will nevertheless apply. In other words, premium leases granted with a significant rent do not benefit from the nil-rate band. The £600 threshold is by reference to 'average annual rent', which is broadly the total stated rent payable throughout the term of the lease divided by the number of years of the term.

5.69 Subject to the above paragraph, where a lease is granted for both rent and a premium, the rates above will apply to the rent element and the rates applicable to transfers and assignments in **Chapters 3** and **4** will apply to the premium. The total SDLT bill for the grant of the lease will be the total of both sums. As a result, the calculation may make use of the nil-rate band for the both the rent and the premium element.

Term of lease

5.70 For the purposes of calculating NPV (and all other purposes relating to SDLT on leases) where a lease is granted after the contractual term commencement date, the term for SDLT purposes commences on the date of grant. Where an agreement for lease is substantially performed but not yet completed by the grant of a lease, and subsequently a lease is granted pursuant to the agreement for lease, the term of the lease commences on the date of substantial performance of the agreement for lease.[45] Accordingly, where an agreement for lease is substantially performed prior to the grant of a lease (for example, in relation to a development agreement where the tenant gains access to carry out works but no lease is granted until completion of the work) there may be difficulty in measuring the term for the purposes of the NPV calculation. This calculation will be needed at the time of substantial performance of the agreement for lease, as a land transaction return will be due within 30 days of that date. This problem is likely to be common in a development scenario where the contractual term of the lease will run from the date of grant, but for SDLT purposes the term will include (in addition to the contractual term) the period between the access date and the date of grant, which is a flexible period. In other agreement for lease scenarios, the contractual term commencement date and the date of grant are less likely to differ. The authors understand that in these circumstances the land transaction return due on substantial performance should be prepared on the basis of a lease for an indefinite term (see **para 5.71**). It would seem that when a lease is finally granted pursuant to the development agreement any SDLT paid in relation to an unexpected deemed term of a year may be credited according to the 'overlap basis' applicable to surrenders and regrants (see **para 6.04** below).

Leases for an indefinite term

5.71 Periodic tenancies terminable by notice, and any other interest or right terminable by notice, are regarded as leases for an indefinite term.[46] Such leases will

---

45 This principle was originally contained in Sch 5, para 6 but was mistakenly deleted by the Variation Regulations. The Inland Revenue has indicated that this principle should be followed in any event.
46 Sch 17A, para 4(1).

be treated as being for a fixed term of a year until their first year of actual duration and a return will need to be submitted within 30 days of the start of such deemed term.[47] If the lease continues for a second year, the lease will be treated as a two-year lease, and so on (ie effectively linking the successive years). Clearly, the continuation of the lease for a period of two years will change the amount of SDLT payable unless this was originally envisaged, and thus a new land transaction return will need to be delivered within 30 days of the end of the first deemed fixed term and at the end of each further deemed fixed term. In certain circumstances, this could bring a lease into charge where it had previously been within an exempt band. The Variation Regulations deleted the provisions originally in the Finance Act 2003 treating perpetual leases, leases for life and leases determinable on the marriage of the lessee as leases for an indefinite term, which leaves the treatment of these in doubt. As these leases are deemed fixed term leases by various legislative provisions[48] the authors' view is that as a result of the Variation Regulations these leases are treated as leases for a fixed term. The authors understand that the provisions applying to leases for an indefinite term are used to achieve the correct result where the term of a lease is flexible due to substantial performance before grant (see **para 5.70** above).

5.72 Fixed-term leases containing a rolling break right would not be regarded as leases for an indefinite term.

5.73 If a lease that continues for an indefinite term is assigned, the assignee takes over responsibility for any further SDLT that becomes payable

---

47 Sch 17A, para 4(3).
48 A lease for a life or lives determinable on marriage takes effect as a lease for 90 years determinable after the death or marriage of the original tenant (s 149(6) Law of Property Act 1925). Perpetually renewable leases are converted into a term of 2,000 years pursuant to Sch 15, para 5 of the Law of Property Act 1922.

by virtue of the continuation of the lease and filing a revised land transaction return.[49]

5.74 Example:

A tenant is allowed into possession under a periodic tenancy, paying monthly rent in advance of each month it is allowed to occupy. As soon as the lease commences, the tenant will have to account for SDLT on the assumption that it will continue in occupation for a year. Thus, if the tenancy began on 1 January 2004, the tenant will have to file a land transaction return with SDLT calculated at 1% of the year's rent (less any exempt amount) by 31 January 2004. If the tenancy continues one day beyond 31 December 2004, the tenant will be obliged to file a further land transaction return within 30 days, accounting for such further amount of SDLT as corresponds to the unpaid amount calculated on a two-year lease.

Leases that continue after a fixed term

5.75 A lease which may continue beyond the original fixed term, whether by agreement or by operation of law (for example by virtue of section 24 of the Landlord and Tenant Act 1954), if it in fact continues after the end of that term, is treated as a lease for a term of one year more than the original fixed term.[50] In other words, the fixed term and the deemed lease for a year's term are treated as linked. Thus if the lease continues only for a day beyond the original fixed term, it will be treated as granted for a term of one year beyond the original fixed term. If the lease continues for more than a year beyond the original fixed term, then it will be deemed a lease for a term two years longer than the original fixed term and so on. Once the deemed term has arisen (in this case, on the continuation beyond

---

49 Sch 17A, para 12(1).
50 Sch 17A, para 3(2).

the end of the original fixed term even for as little as one day) a new land trans-action return will need to be delivered to the Inland Revenue within 30 days of the end of the original fixed term. Again, if the lease continues for more than a year beyond the original fixed term, a revised land transaction return will need to be submitted within 30 days of the end of the first deemed fixed term. The provision does not have effect in relation to the fixed term of leases granted prior to 1 December 2003. It should be noted that there is no right to reclaim SDLT if occupation does not continue for a full year.

5.76 If a lease continues after a fixed term, and such lease is assigned, the respon-sibility for any further SDLT that becomes payable, and for filing a revised land transaction return as a result of such continuation, falls on the assignee.[51]

5.77 Example:

If, on the expiry of a 15-year business tenancy commencing on 1 December 2003, the tenant holds over for a number of days under the Landlord and Tenant Act 1954 or pend-ing negotiations for a renewed lease, the tenant will have to submit a revised return with tax calculated on the NPV of rents passing over a period of 16 years. This is because the tenant will be deemed to have taken a new lease of a year on holding over, which is a trans-action linked with the 15-year term which has terminated. The tenant will have to submit a revised land transaction return within 30 days of the end of the original fixed term.

How do I account for SDLT on a lease?

5.78 As the land transaction is the grant, rather than the transfer or assignment of a lease, code L should be inserted in Box 2. Depending on the type of lease

---

51 Sch 17A, para 12(1).

granted, enter code LG for a long lease with vacant possession, LT for a long lease subject to a lease to an occupier, LP for a lease to an occupier or OT for any other case in Box 3. Code LT may be relevant to the grant of a lease in an overriding lease scenario. A long lease is generally taken to mean a lease granted for a premium with a ground rent rather than a market rent. Box 16 should be completed with either Residential: R, Non-Residential: N or Mixed: M. Boxes 16-25 should then be completed with details of the lease. In the case of commercial leases, SDLT4 will also need to be completed which requests further details about the lease. Form SDLT4 is relatively self-explanatory, but the following points should be noted:

1. Box 9 – *Any terms surrendered* does not refer to the release of specific terms, but is aimed at where a lease has been surrendered in return for the grant of a new lease. Key terms of the lease surrendered should be inserted here.

2. Box 12 – *Which of the following relate to the lease?* an uncertain rent which is not a turnover rent is likely to arise in the case of shared rental leases, geared leases and side-by-side lettings.

5.79 Fuller details of how to complete the land transaction return may be found in the **Appendix**, below.

Is any ongoing compliance necessary?

5.80 The regime applicable to rent increases and to leases granted for a contingent, uncertain or unascertained consideration means that a long list of events will require a reassessment of the consideration payable and the possible obligation to file a revised land transaction return accounting for additional SDLT, and in some situations claiming a refund of SDLT with interest. Some of these events are as follows:

1. A rent review taking effect within the first five years of the term of the lease – reassessment following the rent review or (if not yet determined by then) at the end of the first five years of the term.

2. An abnormal increase after the first five years of the term – this would include an abnormal stepped increase provided for in the lease.

3. The happening of a contingency within the first five years of the term, or it becoming clear that such contingency will not occur – a revised land transaction return will be due on that event or at the end of the fifth year of the term if the effect of this event has not been determined earlier. File an amended revised return once this is determined.

4. An event as a result of which uncertain or unascertained rent payable in the first five years becomes certain, for example the finalisation of turnover accounts in the case of a turnover lease. In such a case, unless the event coincides with the end of the fifth year of the term, the revised return would not be submitted until the end of the fifth year, as the entire rent during the first five years of the lease remains uncertain at that time.

5. In the case of leases for an indefinite term and leases that continue after a fixed term, it will be necessary to monitor the continuation of the tenancy and to diarise when a revised land transaction return will be due with extra tax.

As with any other land transaction, the grant of a lease requires certain key documents to be retained, generally speaking those necessary to support the manner in which the return was completed. This explained in further detail in **Chapter 14**.

6. OTHER LEASE TRANSACTIONS

Lease variations

6.01 A variation of a lease which has the effect of increasing the amount of rent is treated as a grant of a new lease for the consideration of the additional rent, unless the provision for increasing rent is already contained in the lease.[1] This does not apply to the variation of leases granted before 1 December 2003.

Lease surrenders

[handwritten: not sure this is correct]

6.02 In a straightforward situation where a tenant surrenders a lease to a landlord *[handwritten: See eg Rev manuals]* in return for a premium payable by the landlord, the premium will be liable to SDLT at the rates applicable to transfers, (1, 3 or 4%) depending on the size of the premium.[2] However, where a tenant surrenders a lease to a landlord and pays the landlord a premium to take back the lease, (ie a 'reverse surrender') no SDLT charge will arise.[3]

Surrender and regrants

6.03 Where a lease is surrendered to a landlord and a new lease is granted to the tenant, whether of the same or of a different property, the effect of the Variation Regulations is that the transaction is not treated as an exchange. Accordingly, the value of the old lease is not treated as consideration for the grant of the new lease, and the new lease is not treated as consideration for the surrender. It should be noted that

---

1 Sch 17A, para 13.
2 S 43(3)(b).
3 Sch 4, para 15(1).

there are two transactions for SDLT purposes.[4] However, any premium paid either for the surrender or any premium/rent paid for the new lease is subject to SDLT unless an exemption applies. The relief also applies to pre-1 December 2003 leases. The authors understand that the exchange box should not be ticked on the SDLT1.

6.04 Where a lease is surrendered to a landlord in consideration of the landlord granting a new lease to the tenant, any rent payable under the new lease is reduced for SDLT purposes by the rent payable in the 'overlap period'.[5] The overlap period is the period between the date of grant of the new lease and what would have been the end of the term of the old lease had it not been terminated. In order for this to apply, the new lease must relate to 'the same or substantially the same premises'. These provisions also apply where the tenant under a lease of premises subject to Part 2 of the Landlord and Tenant Act 1954 makes a request for a new tenancy which is then executed. The overlap basis does not apply to premiums. The provisions are also relevant to the continuation of fixed-term leases under the 1954 Act where SDLT is payable by reference to a full year of continuation. In these circumstances, overlap relief should be claimed when a new lease is granted.

6.05 The authors understand that the surrender of a lease granted prior to 1 December 2003 cannot benefit from the overlap basis.

6.06 Example:

A landlord wishes to take back an existing lease of a property, grant a new lease on modern commercial terms and include a small annex in the demise. The existing lease has

---

4 And thus both the landlord and the tenant will need to consider whether a return is required.
5 Sch 17A, para 9.

five years left of the term to run. The existing lease was granted for an annual rent of £50,000 and for a term of 25 years. If the new lease is granted for 15 years (ie an additional term of ten years) and for a rent of £75,000 per annum, it will be necessary to calculate the NPV of the 15-year term (£863,805) and subtract the NPV of the five-year 'overlap period' calculated on the rents payable under the existing lease (£112,876), giving a chargeable NPV of £750,929 (£863,805 minus £112,876). If the lease surrendered had value, for example, the rent was below market rent or contained non-market terms beneficial to the tenant, this value would not be taken into account as consideration for the grant of the new lease.

Sale and leaseback transactions

6.07 A sale and leaseback transaction would ordinarily give rise to two charges to SDLT; one on the sale and a second on the leaseback. The SDLT regime relieves the leaseback element from SDLT if the following conditions are fulfilled:[6]

- the property is commercial;
- the sale consideration consists of nothing other than cash or the assumption, satisfaction or release of a debt; and
- the leaseback relates to the same premises as the sale.

It should be noted that the relief does not apply where the leaseback is not to the same entity as the transferor, even if that entity is a connected party. Whilst the leaseback would generally be made for rent consideration only, the legislation would seem to suggest that any premium consideration for the leaseback would also be exempt.

---

6 S 57A.

6.08 Example:

A retailer agrees to sell valuable premises to an investment bank for £8m satisfied as to £5m in cash and as to £3m by the assumption of debts of the retailer in return for a lease-back of the property. The rent payable on the leaseback of the property has an NPV of £9m. The sale transaction will incur SDLT at the rate of 4% on the £8m consideration but no charge will arise in the hands of the retailer on the leaseback.

6.09 Lease exchanges which are not surrender and regrant or sale and leaseback transactions are dealt with according to the rules in **paras 3.41-3.47**.

7. Non-monetary consideration

7.01 As mentioned in **Chapter 2**, the legislation includes a wide definition of chargeable consideration, which can include many categories of non-monetary consideration. Any consideration in money or money's worth will be chargeable.

7.02 Under the stamp duty regime, the non-monetary consideration which was taken into account was generally limited to shares, debt and land provided in exchange. For SDLT purposes any non-monetary consideration, whether in the form of goods or services, is chargeable and specific provisions are made for debt, construction works, leasehold obligations and land provided in exchange.

Valuation of non-monetary consideration

7.03 The value of non-monetary consideration for the purposes of SDLT is the market value of such consideration at the effective date of the transaction.[1] Debt is excluded from this rule, as it is valued according to its own specific rules.

Debt consideration

7.04 Debt can constitute or add to the chargeable consideration for a land transaction in any of the following circumstances:[2]

1. where the vendor transfers land to the purchaser to satisfy or release a debt *due to the purchaser*, the purchaser will be regarded as having paid consideration equivalent to the debt satisfied or released;

---

1 Sch 4, para 7.
2 Sch 4, para 8(1).

2. where the vendor transfers land to satisfy or release a debt *owed by the vendor,* the purchaser will be regarded as having paid consideration equivalent to the debt satisfied or released; and

3. where the vendor transfers land to the purchaser in return for the purchaser assuming existing debt owed by the vendor to a third party,[3] the purchaser will be regarded as having paid consideration equivalent to the amount of the debt assumed by it.

7.05 The amount of the debt which falls into charge as chargeable consideration is the total of the principal amount payable, together with any interest that has accrued due on or before the effective date of the transaction.[4]

7.06 There is, however, a cap on the amount of consideration which can be constituted by debt. If the total consideration including the debt and any other items payable for the chargeable interest which is the subject matter of the transaction (ie the land) exceeds the market value of that interest, the total chargeable consideration is capped at that market value.[5]

7.07 Generally, where a property subject to a mortgage is sold, the vendor will discharge the outstanding mortgage just before the purchaser acquires the property, and the purchaser will then secure its own mortgage on the property. In these circumstances, there is no assumption of debt. However, using the example given in the SDLT Manual[6], where A and B jointly own a property which is mortgaged and A pays B to buy out B's interest, the chargeable consideration will comprise the amount paid and the share of the outstanding mortgage debt assumed by A.

---

3 Sch 4, para 8(3)(b).
4 Sch 4, para 8(3)(c).
5 Sch 4, para 8(2).
6 Para 4040a.

Provision of services

7.08 The value of any services carried out in consideration of a land transaction is brought into account in the calculation of chargeable consideration.[7] The relevant test of value is the amount that would have to be paid in the open market to obtain such services. While there was some concern that the service of building maintenance and other services provided under Private Finance Initiative contracts would be regarded as chargeable consideration, in response to a consultation on this and other issues relating to complex commercial transactions, provisions were inserted in Schedule 4 by the Stamp Duty Land Tax (Amendment of Schedule 4 to the Finance Act 2003) Regulations 2003[8] which have the effect of disregarding such works and services as chargeable consideration (see **para 9.75**). However, a separate rule applies to construction works.

Construction works

7.09 The practical application of the principles discussed below relating to works consideration is discussed further in **Chapter 12** below. The following points set out the basic principles.

7.10 Where construction works are carried out constituting the whole or part of the consideration for a land transaction, in certain circumstances the value of the construction works will constitute, or be added to, the chargeable consideration.[9] The relevant value to be taken into account is that which would have to be paid in the open market for the carrying out of the works in question.

---

7 Sch 4, para 11.
8 SI 2003/3293.
9 Sch 4, para 10.

7.11 The rule applies to 'works of construction, improvement or repair of a building or other works to enhance the value of land'.

7.12 The rules apply to works carried out or commissioned by the purchaser. It would appear from clarification provided by the Inland Revenue that the charge on building works carried out by or commissioned by a vendor remains unaffected by these provisions, as the legislation only relates to works carried out in consideration for a land transaction. The legislation thus does not deal with the *Prudential v IRC*[10] rule which brings the value of construction works carried out by or on behalf of the vendor into charge in certain circumstances. This rule is discussed in **Chapter 12**.

7.13 Unless all the following conditions can be met, the relevant works will constitute chargeable consideration:

1. the works are carried out after the effective date of the transaction;
2. the works are carried out on land acquired or to be acquired under the transaction or on other land held by the purchaser or a person connected with it; and
3. it is not a condition of the transaction that the works are carried out by the vendor or a person connected with it.

The first consequence of this provision is that where a purchaser carries out works on other land owned by the vendor as part of the consideration for a land transaction, this will constitute chargeable consideration. The second consequence is that if the works are to be carried out on land which is the subject of the

---

10 [1992] STC 863.

transaction, but they will be carried out before the effective date of the land transaction, the value of the works will fall into charge. The final consequence is that, even if the works are carried out after the effective date of the transaction and they are carried out on land acquired under the transaction, but it is a condition of the transaction that the vendor or a person connected with the vendor carries out the works, the value of the works will nevertheless be taken into account as chargeable consideration.

7.14 The authors understand that, in a situation where the contract provides for the purchaser to carry out building works before sale or lease, a charge should arise on the value of the construction works. The reason for this is that, generally speaking, the purchaser will have substantially performed the contract when it (or a builder on its behalf) is given access to the land to carry out the works. It should be possible, therefore, to say that the works are carried out after the effective date of the transaction, and provided the other conditions are met, the works should not fall into charge. Nevertheless, it needs to be remembered that a further land transaction is deemed to occur on completion. The authors understand that, in these circumstances, the works consideration has been exempted and cannot fall into charge again under a second land transaction. However, this conclusion may not apply if the transaction, entered into on completion provides for the works consideration. This issue is discussed further in **Chapter 12**.

7.15 Example 1:

A agrees to sell a property to B for £2m. In addition and as part of the transaction B agrees to do works on other land owned by A. The market value of those works is £1m. B must pay duty at 4% of £3m (plus relevant VAT).

7.16 Example 2:

A agrees to sell a property to B for £2m. In addition and as part of the transaction, B agrees to do works after completion to the value of £1m. The works are carried out partly on the property purchased and partly on the land owned by A. The value of the works is £1m, of which £300,000 is properly attributable to the works carried out on the other land owned by A. SDLT will be due on £2.3m.

7.17 Example 3:

A agrees to sell a property to B for £2m. In addition and as part of the transaction B agrees to carry out works on the property purchased after completion to the value of £1m. It is a condition of the contract that the works are to be carried out by a subsidiary of B. B must pay SDLT on a consideration of £3m.

Other specific charges on non-monetary consideration

7.18 Where a land transaction is entered into by reason of employment, an SDLT charge will arise if and to the extent that the land transaction constitutes a taxable benefit for income tax purposes and such charge is imposed on the basis of a deemed rent.[11] For example, if an employer allows an employee to occupy a flat owned by the employer for a rent of £200 per week when the market rent would be £250 per week, the employee will have to pay lease duty on the basis of a rent of £250 per week.

7.19 Certain leasehold obligations can constitute services which will be treated as chargeable consideration. In the case of a grant of a lease, the

---

11 Sch 4, para 12.

following obligations in the lease will not constitute chargeable consideration:[12]

1. undertakings by the tenant to repair, maintain or insure the demised premises;

2. undertakings by the tenant to pay any amount in respect of services, repairs, maintenance or insurance or the landlord's costs of management;

3. guarantees of the payment of rent or the performance of any other obligation of the tenant under the lease; or

4. penal rents (or increased rents in the nature of penal rents) payable in respect of the breach of any obligation of the tenant under the lease.

7.20 There is a further catch-all exclusion for 'any other obligation undertaken by the tenant that is not such as to affect the rent that a tenant would be prepared to pay in the open market'.[13] This provision would appear to require a valuer to examine every lease clause, such as keep-open covenants and other trade stipulations, to see whether such clauses would affect the rent. While this would seem to open up a large area of complexity, indications from the Inland Revenue are that its general aim is not to bring lease clauses into account for the purpose of calculating chargeable consideration. It would seem that the usual range of user covenants and restrictions on assignment do not need to be reported or taken into account. In the case of highly unusual clauses, it may be necessary to discuss with the Inland Revenue whether these might add to the chargeable consideration.

7.21 As regards the assignment of a leasehold interest, the assumption by the assignee of any of the obligations of the tenant (in particular, the obligation to pay

---

12 Sch 17A, para 10.
13 Sch 17A, para 10(1)(c).

rent) is excluded from constituting chargeable consideration.[14] The same applies in the case of a surrender. The legislation does not specify that the assumption of obligations in relation to leases to which the interest sold is subject are exempt in any way. Theoretically there may be an issue where a freehold interest or lease-hold interest subject to lettings is sold, and the purchaser takes over the obligation to pursue arrears of rent, undertake a rent review or to indemnify the vendor in relation to positive covenants. However, these obligations are generally included as market practice and thus are unlikely to have any value.

7.22 Example:

A Ltd owns three shop units but grants a lease to B Ltd containing a non-compete clause. This would be an obligation undertaken by the tenant, but the nature of the obligation could well be relevant to rent levels and could be taken into account at rent review. The non-compete covenant would most likely affect the rent that a tenant would be prepared to pay in the open market, and thus the effect of this clause would need to be valued and such value would be taken into account in calculating lease duty.

Powers of appointment and exercise of discretion

7.23 The legislation contains specific rules to deem consideration to be paid on the exercise of a power of appointment or the exercise of a discretion vested in trustees.[15] When either is exercised, any consideration given by or on behalf of the person in whose favour the appointment was made or the discretion was exercised in order to become an object of the power or discretion, is treated as consideration for that exercise.

---

14 Sch 17A, para 17.
15 Sch 16, para 7.

7.24 Example:

Mr A is a beneficiary under a discretionary trust which holds a valuable property among other assets. The trustees have no current plans to dispose of the property. Mr A wants to purchase the property and he pays the trustees and/or the other beneficiaries market value for the property on the basis of an understanding that the trustees will exercise their discretion in his favour. The trustees later exercise their discretion to appoint the property in Mr A's favour. This will not serve to avoid SDLT, as the amount paid by Mr A will be treated as consideration for the acquisition of the property by Mr A on exercise of the trustees' discretion.

Annuities

7.25 When the consideration for a land transaction consists of an annuity payable: (a) for life; (b) in perpetuity; (c) for an indefinite period; or (d) for a definite period exceeding 12 years, only 12 years' annual payment is taken into account.[16] Where the amount payable varies, or may vary from year to year, the 12 highest annual payments are used. If the annuity provides for increases in line with the Retail Price Index, these increases are ignored. In many cases it will not be possible to tell at the effective date how much annuity consideration will fall into charge, and accordingly the rules applicable to contingent, uncertain and unascertained consideration will apply and a reviewed land transaction return will be due each time the amount of one or more annuity payments become certain. In limiting the number of annual payments that is taken into account, the 12-year period begins with the effective date of the transaction.

---

16 S 52(1).

8. SUBSALES

8.01 A subsale occurs where A contracts to sell a property to B and, before a conveyance is executed, B contracts to sell the property to C. Both the contract between A and B and the contract between B and C are completed when A transfers the property to C on receipt of the purchase price. Sometimes these transactions occur with more than two contracts, and subsales are common in a development scenario where a plot is sold to the developer, which is then divided and sold on to particular end-purchasers. Generally, the end-purchaser will pay straight to A the amount payable under the first contract and will pay any excess consideration under its contract with B to B.

8.02 The approach of the legislation is to prevent subsale relief being available (ie a charge arises on both contracts)in situations where the contracts are substantially performed before any transfer is effected to the end-purchaser. This is aimed at preventing avoidance by use of 'resting on contract' split title schemes which relied on subsale relief under the stamp duty regime. These schemes used subsale relief to avoid a charge to stamp duty on a transaction by avoiding any stampable document of transfer, even though full payment had been made and in a commercial sense the transaction had been completed. Subsale relief could be claimed under stamp duty when, eventually, it became necessary to collapse the split titles or pass the titles to a third party. Under the SDLT rules, in these scenarios substantial performance occurs when a purchaser pays the consideration under the contract which is left uncompleted, thereby triggering an SDLT charge.

8.03 In order for subsale relief to be available, there needs to be a contract for a land transaction followed by an assignment, subsale or other transaction (eg a novation) whereby a person other than the original purchaser has the right to call for a conveyance to them.[1] In addition, the following condition ('substantial performance condition') must be fulfilled:[2]

The earlier contract (ie the contract between A and B) must not be substantially performed or completed prior to the substantial performance or completion of the subsequent contract.[3] If there are more than two contracts in the chain, the consideration payable under any contract which is substantially performed or completed prior to the substantial performance or completion of the subsequent contract in the chain will fall into charge.

Thus where there is a contract between A and B, B and C, and C and D, if only the contract between B and C is substantially performed early, this will not prejudice relief in relation to the consideration payable under the contract between A and B.

Where the condition is not fulfilled, the consideration payable under each contract which is substantially performed or completed will fall into charge.

8.04 The end result of the legislation is that subsale relief under the stamp duty regime is to some extent preserved. Where the conditions are fulfilled, SDLT is payable only on the consideration passing under the final contract in the chain. The substantial performance condition means that resting on contract and split title avoidance schemes will no longer be effective. It should be noted, as discussed further in **Chapter 12** that the substantial performance condition makes subsale relief

---

1 S 45(1).
2 A contract would be substantially performed in these circumstances if 90% or more of the consideration under the contract is paid, or the purchaser, or a person on its behalf enters into possession.
3 S 45(3).

unavailable in certain common development scenarios where the developer gains access to carry out works before on-sale to the final purchaser.

A potential pitfall with the substantial performance condition arises in the context of the common arrangement whereby C pays to A an amount equivalent to the consideration passing under the A-B contract, and pays to B the amount of any difference under the B-C contract. In order to prevent a possible early substantial performance of the A-B contract, the payments should be made simultaneously.

In the *SDLT Customer Newsletter* Issue 3, the Inland Revenue confirms the view based on certain transitional provisions[4] that the substantial performance of a contract before 1 December 2003 which is followed by a subsale after 1 December 2003 will not give rise to a charge on the pre-1 December 2003 limb of the subsale. Further details of this are contained in **Chapter 11** regarding transitional provisions.

8.05 The legislation sets out the appropriate basis for subsales of part. Where any part of the land which is the subject matter of a prior contract (ie between A and B) is the subject of a contract between the purchaser under the prior contract and the purchaser under a subsequent contract (ie B and C), an apportionment will need to be carried out in order to determine which portion of the consideration payable under the prior contract is subject to the rule. When the contracts are completed by a conveyance, reassessment of the tax payable may be necessary to the extent the tax payable on the land transaction constituted by the conveyance exceeds any which is payable as a result of any substantially performed contracts.[5]

---

4 Sch 19, para 4(3).
5 S 45(5).

9. SDLT EXEMPTIONS AND RELIEFS

Introduction

9.01 The Finance Act 2003 provides for a number of transactions not to be chargeable to SDLT because of the application of a specific exemption or relief. It should be noted that, generally, the transactions which are exempt from SDLT pursuant to Schedule 3 (detailed in **para 9.03** below) do not require the purchaser to file a land transaction return and all the purchaser will need to do is to self-certify in order to register the interest with the Land Registry. By contrast, the items detailed from **para 9.11** onwards (which for the purposes of this chapter are called reliefs) will generally still require the purchaser to file a land transaction return and to claim the specific relief.

9.02 In addition to the exemptions and reliefs detailed in this chapter it must be borne in mind that certain transactions are not within the scope of SDLT. This includes transactions involving non-UK land, licences, security interests and (certainly until the Finance Act 2004) acquisitions and disposals of land into and out of partnerships by partners and transfers of partnership interests. Furthermore, if the consideration does not exceed the appropriate nil-rate band, or is otherwise excluded from being chargeable consideration, then no SDLT will be payable. These issues are covered elsewhere in the book.

Summary of exemptions and reliefs

Table 10A

Exempt transactions

Description	FA 2003 provision	Previous stamp duty provision
Transactions where there is no chargeable consideration	Schedule 3, paragraph 1	Categories (A)-(G), (I)-(L)[1]
Transactions in contemplation of or in connection with divorce or separation	Schedule 3, paragraph 3	Category H[2]
Variation of testamentary dispositions, etc	Schedule 3, paragraph 4	Category M[3]
Certain grants of leases by registered social landlords	Schedule 3, paragraph 2	Section 128 FA 2003

Table 10B

Reliefs

Description	FA 2003 provision	Previous stamp duty provision	Code for Box 9 land transaction return
Acquisition relief	Section 62 and Schedule 7, Part 2	Section 76 FA 1986	14
Alternative property finance	Sections 72 and 73	None	24
Bodies established for national purposes	Section 69	Section 129 FA 1982	21
Charities	Section 68 and Schedule 8	Section 129 FA 1982	20
Collective enfranchisement by leaseholders	Section 74	None	25
Compliance with planning obligations	Section 61	None	11
Compulsory purchase facilitating development	Section 60	None	10
Crofting community right to buy	Section 75	None	26
Crown purchases	Section 107	Section 55 FA 1987	28

---

1 Sch to the Stamp Duty (Exempt Instrument) Regulations 1987 (SI 1987/516), reg 4.

2 *Ibid.*

3 *Ibid.*

Table 10B (cont)			
Reliefs			
Description	**FA 2003 Provision**	**Previous stamp duty provision**	**Code for box 9 land transaction return**
Demutualisation of building society	Section 64	Section 109 Building Societies Act 1986	16
Demutualisation of insurance company	Section 63	Section 96 FA 1997	15
Disadvantaged areas	Section 57 and Schedule 6	Section 92 and Schedule 30 FA 2001	05 – residential 06 – commercial 07 – mixed
Group relief	Section 62 and Schedule 7, Part 1	Section 42 FA 1930 and Section 151 FA 1995	12
Incorporation of limited liability partnership	Section 65	Section 12 Limited Liability Partnerships Act 2000	17
Parliamentary constituency reorganisation	Section 67	Section 7 Finance (No 2) Act 1983	19
Private Finance Initiative arrangements	Schedule 4, paragraph 17	None	28
Reconstruction relief	Section 62 and Schedule 7, part 2	Section 75 FA 1986	13
Registered social landlords	Section 71	Section 130 FA 2000	23
Relocation of employment	Section 58A and Schedule 6A	None	09
Residential property acquisitions	Section 58A and Schedule 6A	None	08 and 28
Right-to-buy transactions, shared-ownership leases, etc	Section 70 and Schedule 9	Section 97 FA 1980 and Section 107 FA 1981	22
Statutory reorganisation of public bodies	Section 66	None	18
Unit trust initial transfers	Section 64A	None	28

Exempt transactions

9.03 The following transactions are specifically exempted from charge:

1. transactions for no consideration;[4]

---

4 Sch 3, para 1.

2.   grant of leases by registered social landlords;[5]

3.   transactions in connection with divorce;[6] and

4.   variations of testamentary dispositions.[7]

In all these cases, the 30-day reporting requirement[8] does not apply but the purchaser will need to self-certify[9] that no land transaction return is due in order to register the interest with the Land Registry.[10]

Transactions for no consideration

9.04 A land transaction is exempt if there is no chargeable consideration. This means that the following will be exempt:

1.   gifts (note however that transfers of land to a connected company are deemed to be for a market value consideration);[11]

2.   testamentary dispositions;

3.   dispositions under intestacy law;

4.   dispositions of property to beneficiaries under a trust;

5.   most acquisitions by operation of law;

6.   a distribution of property to shareholders by a company on its winding up;[12]

7.   a dividend *in specie* of property to shareholders of a company, provided that

---

5 Sch 3, para 2.
6 Sch 3, para 3.
7 Sch 3, para 4.
8 S 77.
9 S 79(3).
10 S 79(3).
11 S 53.
12 The market value rule of s 53 for connected company transfers does not apply to distributions: s 54(4).

the distribution does not involve the assumption of liabilities or is not in satisfaction of a liability;[13]

8. the appointment of a new trustee to a trust, including in respect of a pension fund;

9. an appropriation of assets of an estate under section 41 of the Administration of Estates Act 1925;[14] and

10. where property is conveyed from the trustees of one pension fund to another pension fund, provided the only consideration given is the assumption by the new fund of obligations to provide retirement benefits. In addition the Inland Revenue has stated that if the new fund assumes an existing liability of the old fund to repay borrowings as part and parcel of the transfer, then this will not be treated as chargeable consideration.[15]

Most of the transactions covered by this exemption were specifically exempted from stamp duty by one of the categories in the Schedule to the Stamp Duty (Exempt Instrument) Regulations 1987.

9.05 Example:

A agrees to transfer a freehold to B for no payment. The freehold is subject to a mortgage. B assumes this mortgage obligation and, therefore, has given chargeable consideration. The transfer is not exempt and a land transaction return should be lodged.

---

13 *Ibid.*
14 The view that such a transaction would be exempt is included in a note approved by the Inland Revenue set out in Issue 3942 (29 January 2004) of *Taxation* on p 413.
15 The position of the Inland Revenue is to be included in the SDLT Manual, but is set out in Issue 727 (9 February 2004) of the *Tax Journal* on p 18.

Grant of certain leases by registered social landlords

9.06 This is an exemption for the tenant rather than for the registered social landlord.[16] The grant of a lease of a dwelling is exempt from charge if:

1. the lease is granted by a registered social landlord to one or more individuals;

2. it is in accordance with an arrangement between a registered social landlord and a housing authority under which the landlord provides, for individuals nominated by the authority pursuant to its statutory housing functions, temporary rented accommodation which the landlord itself has obtained on a short-term basis (for these purposes, a lease is granted on a short-term basis if it is accommodation leased to the landlord for a term of five years or less); and

3. the lease is for an indefinite term or is terminable by notice of a month or less.

9.07 For the purposes of this exemption a 'housing authority' is a local authority council and in relation to Northern Ireland 'housing authority' includes the Department for Social Development in Northern Ireland and the Northern Ireland Housing Executive. There is a separate relief available to registered social landlords for certain acquisitions, which is dealt with in **para 9.95**.

Transactions in connection with divorce

9.08 A transaction made in connection with the end of a marriage is exempt from SDLT if it is effected:

1. in pursuance of an order of a court made in respect of a decree of divorce, nullity or marriage or judicial separation; or

---

16 Defined in s 121.

2. in pursuance of an order of a court made in connection with a dissolution or annulment of the marriage, or the parties' judicial separation, at any time after the granting of such decree; or

3. in pursuance or an order of a court made at any time under sections 22A, 23A or 24A of the Matrimonial Causes Act 1973; or

4. in pursuance of an incidental order of a court made under section 8(2) of the Family Law (Scotland) Act 1985 by virtue of section 14(1) of that Act; or

5. at any time in pursuance of an agreement of parties made in contemplation or otherwise in connection with the dissolution or annulment of the marriage, their judicial separation or the making of a separation order in respect of them.

This exemption follows category H of the Stamp Duty (Exempt Instruments) Regulations 1987. The transaction will not be exempt where the parties are not married, ie where the relationship is *de facto*.

Variation of testamentary dispositions

9.09 A transaction following a person's death that varies a disposition, whether by a will or by the law relating to intestacy, of property which the deceased was competent to dispose of is exempt from SDLT provided that:

1. the transaction is carried out within the period of two years after the person's death; and

2. no consideration in money or money's worth other than the making of a variation of another such disposition is given for it.

Note that this exemption applies whether or not the administration of the estate is complete or the property has been distributed in accordance with the original dispositions. This exemption follows category M of the Stamp Duty (Exempt Instruments) Regulations 1987.

Power to add further exemptions

9.10 The SDLT regime provides that the Treasury may make further regulations exempting any description of land transaction from charge to SDLT.

Disadvantaged areas relief

9.11 Disadvantaged areas relief was introduced in the Finance Act 2001. This originally provided that if a conveyance or lease of land could be certified as having taken place in a 'disadvantaged area' and the value of the land was £150,000 or less, no stamp duty would be chargeable.

9.12 Once the European Commission had ruled that to remove the £150,000 cap in the case of commercial land would not constitute state aid, the Chancellor was free to remove the cap in respect of commercial land on 10 April 2003.[17] Thus, land transactions in disadvantaged areas taking place after that date that relate to commercial property will not be liable to any stamp duty or SDLT.

9.13 The disadvantaged areas are designated by regulation[18] according to two methods, wards and postcodes. Land will be regarded as in a disadvantaged area if:

---

17 Stamp Duty (Disadvantaged Areas) (Application of Exemptions) Regulations 2003, SI 2003/1056. The present EC ruling expires on 31 December 2006. The state aid rules will then come under fresh review which may have implications for the scope of the relief.
18 Stamp Duty (Disadvantaged Areas) Regulations 2001, SI 2001/3747 ('Disadvantaged Areas Regulations').

1. as at 7 May 1998 the land fell within one of the wards and electoral divisions listed in the Disadvantaged Areas Regulations then the land will be entitled to the relief; or

2. the land as at 27 November 2001 had a postcode which was identical to the full postcode of land which as at 7 May 1998 did fall within one of those wards and electoral divisions, then the land will be entitled to the relief.

9.14 In order to find out whether land is in a disadvantaged area it is therefore necessary to check whether **1.** or **2.** above are fulfilled. Where there is a postcode available for the site, the first step is to check, by using the Inland Revenue's online search tool,[19] that the postcode is one which would be treated as disadvantaged at the relevant time. However, this should be treated only as an initial indication. The postcode applying to the land may have changed since 27 November 2001, and further, due to certain difficulties with the search facility, at the time of writing the Inland Revenue does not guarantee the results of the search tool. Also, sometimes there will be no postcode, as is common in the case of bare land, or in the case of Northern Ireland, which is not covered by the postcode search. Therefore, it will usually be necessary to check whether the land is in a disadvantaged ward as listed in the Disadvantaged Areas Regulations. The difficulty is that the boundaries of wards are subject to change and the current ward maps may not reflect the position as at 7 May 1998. For this reason, the Inland Revenue refers to the ward maps appearing on the 'neighbourhood statistics' section of the Office of National Statistics (ONS) website[20] and states that these can be relied upon for the purpose of deciding the boundaries of a ward or electoral division for the purposes of the relief. It is nevertheless advisable to check with the Inland Revenue in the run-up to a transaction that the ONS maps can still be relied upon. If the ONS maps cannot be relied upon for this reason, or a

---

19 See: www.inlandrevenue.gov.uk/so/pcode_search.htm
20 See: www.neighbourhood.statistics.gov.uk

more detailed map is necessary, the only option will be to obtain a ward map from the relevant local authority, which states the position as at 7 May 1998.

Residential/commercial

9.15 Since the removal of the cap in relation to commercial property, it is essential to decide whether the land in question is residential or commercial for the purposes of the relief. (See **para 2.32** which provides a fuller definition of the distinction between residential and commercial property.)

9.16 The legislation makes the distinction between commercial and residential property by defining residential property, and any property that does not fit within this definition is 'non-residential' (herein termed commercial).

9.17 The main definition of 'residential property' is a building that is used or suitable for use as a dwelling, or is in the process of being constructed or adapted for such a use.[21] Any garden or grounds belonging to the land or any interests or right subject to it will also be treated as residential. There are also further categories of residential property such as residential accommodation for school pupils and residential accommodation for students and the armed forces.[22] However, there is also a list of excluded categories, such as children's homes, students' halls of residence and hospitals.[23] All of these categories are excluded from being regarded as residential, whether or not they may be suitable for other use.[24]

---

21 S 116(1)(a).
22 S 116(2).
23 S 116(3).
24 Where a building that is not in use is suitable for use for at least one of the categories of residential use and at least one of the categories of excluded use, the legislation contains a form of 'tiebreaker' in s 116(5).

9.18 Whether land is suitable for residential or commercial use will be a question of fact. The Inland Revenue Statement of Practice SP 1/03[25] contains detailed guidance as to when property will be regarded as residential and as commercial or mixed. The simple removal of a bathroom suite or kitchen facilities would not render a building unsuitable for use as a dwelling. However, where a building has been substantially altered, it may be regarded as having become a non-residential building, but evidence of this must be shown in order to obtain the complete relief. Where there are distinct parts of the building, so that part of the building is used as a dwelling, the mixed-use provisions described below will apply.

9.19 If the last use of the property was as a dwelling, and since then it has been left vacant, it will be taken to be 'suitable for use as a dwelling'. An office block will not generally be regarded a suitable for use as a dwelling unless it has been adapted for such use.

9.20 Undeveloped land is assumed to be commercial, even if it is acquired with the intention of constructing residential buildings on it, or even if planning permission has already been obtained for such use. However, it may be regarded as residential if a residential building is being built on it at the date of the land transaction. The process of construction is taken as commencing when the builders start work.

9.21 Where an existing building is being adapted or restored to residential use at the date of the land transaction, the land is treated as residential. Again, the process of construction is taken as commencing when the builders start work. This would also apply where a derelict building is being made fit for habitation.

---

25 This Statement of Practice relates to stamp duty, but it is understood that it is being revised for SDLT purposes.

9.22 Where six or more separate dwellings are the subject of a single transaction involving the transfer or lease in respect of a major interest in land, then the dwellings are treated as commercial land,[26] even if the buildings are still in the process of construction at the time of the land transaction. There needs to be a single contract in respect of the six or more dwellings in order for this rule to apply.

9.23 Owing to the way in which the definition of residential land and commercial land is framed, it does not seem possible that disadvantaged area relief can be claimed after the effective date of the transaction if the intention in respect of residential land changes to that of a commercial purpose.

Land wholly within a disadvantaged area[27]

9.24 If the land is wholly commercial, the transaction will be exempt from SDLT.

9.25 If the land is all residential, then provided the consideration for the transaction does not exceed £150,000, or in the case of rent the NPV of the lease does not exceed £150,000, then the transaction is exempt.

9.26 If the land is partly commercial and partly residential, a just and reasonable apportionment of the consideration needs to be made between the consideration attributable to the commercial land and the consideration attributable to the residential land. The consideration attributable to the commercial land is exempt. The consideration attributable to the residential land is exempt if it does not exceed £150,000, or in the case of rent the attributable NPV does not exceed £150,000.

---

26 S 116(7).
27 Sch 6, part 2.

9.27 As with the normal application of the nil-rate band to lease duty, if a lease is for both rent and non-rent consideration, and the annual rent exceeds £600 the lease will be outside the limit for residential property even if the other consideration is £150,000 or less. The other consideration will be subject to SDLT at the rate of 1%.

Land partly within a disadvantaged area[28]

9.28 Where land is situated partly within a disadvantaged area and partly outside it, then the consideration must be apportioned on a just and reasonable basis. Only the consideration attributed to the land which is not entitled to disadvantaged area relief is taken into account for the purposes of the SDLT thresholds, as disadvantaged area relief deems the consideration benefiting from the relief not to be chargeable consideration. If all of the land partly within a disadvantaged area is commercial, then all the consideration attributable to the land is exempt.

9.29 If all the land is residential, then the consideration attributable to the land situated in the disadvantaged area is exempt, provided it does not exceed £150,000 or, in the case of rent, the attributable NPV does not exceed £150,000.

9.30 If the land within the disadvantaged area is partly commercial and partly residential, then a further just and reasonable apportionment is made between the commercial and residential parts and:

1. the consideration attributable to land within the disadvantaged area that is commercial property is exempt;

---

28 Sch 6, part 3.

2. the consideration attributable to land within the disadvantaged area that is residential property is exempt only if it does not exceed £150,000 or, in the case of rent, the attributable NPV does not exceed £150,000.

9.31 As with land which is wholly in a disadvantaged area, where the consideration for the transaction is partly rent and partly other consideration, and the rent exceeds £600, then the exemption available for the residential element will not apply even though the other consideration is £150,000 or less. The other consideration will be subject to SDLT at the rate of 1%.

9.32 Example:

DevCo Ltd contracts to acquire for £300,000 a piece of land on which is built a grocery store and some flats above. In addition to the grocery store and flats is a large area of land to be used as a car park. Part of the car park extends over land which is not in a disadvantaged area, but the remainder of the land (including the buildings) is in a disadvantaged area. 85% of the consideration for the land is attributable to the portion within the disadvantaged area and 30% of that total proportion is attributable to the residential flats, all of which are in the portion of the land which is disadvantaged. The treatment of the consideration is as follows:

Portion of consideration potentially subject to disadvantaged areas relief:

$$85/100 \times £300,000 = £255,000$$

Portion of consideration attributable to non-residential property:

$$70/100 \times £255,000 = £178,500$$

This portion of the consideration will benefit from disadvantaged areas relief and is exempt.

Portion of consideration attributable to residential property:

$$30/100 \times £255,000 = £76,500$$

As this portion of the consideration is not more than £150,000, it will benefit from disadvantaged areas relief. The only proportion of the consideration that is not attributable to the land in the disadvantaged area, ie £45,000, will anyhow not fall into charge, as it is below the 1% threshold.

Alternatively, DevCo Ltd does not take a transfer of the land, but takes a long lease for the same premium subject to a ground rent attributable to the land in the disadvantaged area of £5,000 per annum. Even though the portion of the premium attributable to residential property in the land situated in a disadvantaged area is only £76,500, since 30% of the ground rent attributable to the residential land is £1,500, the entire consideration attributable to the residential property will not benefit from disadvantaged areas relief. The rent and the premium attributable would be subject to a charge at 1% of the NPV of the ground rents throughout the term of the lease and the entire £76,500 proportion of the premium.

Claiming disadvantaged areas relief

9.33 In relation to transactions before 1 December 2003, disadvantaged areas relief was claimed for stamp duty purposes upon adjudication by inserting an appropriate certificate in the contract or in the letter claiming adjudication. From 1 December 2003, such a certificate is not needed and disadvantaged areas relief is claimed in the land transaction return by inserting codes (05 – residential), (06 – non-residential) or (07 – mixed) in Box 9 for whichever form of disadvantaged areas relief is being claimed.

Group relief

Background

9.34 The stamp duty exemptions for the transfer of property[29] or the grant of a lease[30] between companies in common ownership have in large measure been reproduced into the SDLT code by Part 1, Schedule 7.

Thus SDLT is not chargeable if the vendor and the purchaser are companies which are members of the same group on the effective date of the transaction. Group relief is, however, subject to strict anti-avoidance provisions, and the relief is clawed back if, broadly, the purchaser company leaves the group within three years of the effective date.

If the relief applies, then what would otherwise be a chargeable transaction involving the transfer of a freehold or leasehold interest, or the grant of a new lease, will be exempt from SDLT.[31]

Company

9.35 For the purposes of this relief 'company' means a body corporate, wherever incorporated or resident, and thus the relief is available to non-UK companies without restriction. A body corporate does not include a partnership or a group of trustees and requires the entity in question to have a separate legal personality, perpetual succession and the ability to own separate rights and assets. Although

---

29 Finance Act 1930, s 42.
30 Finance Act 1995, s 151.
31 Sch 7, para 1(1).

the parent company need not have a share capital (and thus can include companies limited by guarantee and probably limited liability partnerships) the other members of the group must have a share capital or, for companies incorporated outside the UK, rights equivalent to a share capital. The Inland Revenue does provide a list of foreign entities which they consider qualify as a company for these purposes.[32]

Group tests

9.36 For the purposes of the relief, companies are members of the same group if one is the 75% subsidiary of the other or both are 75% subsidiaries of a third company. The 75% subsidiary test looks first at the actual ownership of ordinary share capital and requires that one company must be the beneficial owner of a least 75% of the ordinary share capital of the other company. 'Ordinary share capital' is defined as all the issued share capital of a company other than shares carrying a right to a fixed dividend with no other right to participate in the company's profits.[33] This test looks only at the nominal value of the company's ordinary share capital and not at the market value of the shares.[34]

Care must be taken to ensure that, at the effective date, beneficial ownership of a relevant shareholding has not been lost. This could arise, for example, if the parent company has contracted to sell the subsidiary outside the group or, possibly, if the parent company has gone into liquidation on or before the effective date of the transaction. Where a third party has been granted an option to acquire shares in the subsidiary, this should not generally cause beneficial ownership to be

---

32 Inland Revenue Stamp Office Manual 2003, para 6.124.
33 Sch 7, para 1(5).
34 This is based on the stamp duty case of *Canada Safeway Ltd v IRC* [1972] 1 All ER 666.

lost, except perhaps if the arrangement deprives the parent of the right to enjoy dividends.[35]

9.37 In determining whether 75% or more of ordinary share capital is held by a particular company, indirect holdings are counted and fractional entitlement through a chain of companies is determined by multiplying the fractions in the chain.[36]

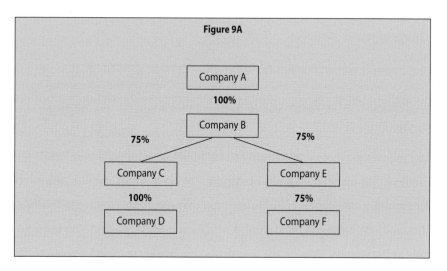

Figure 9A

In the above example, Company A, Company B, Company C, Company D and Company E are all members of the same group for SDLT purposes. However, Company F is not a member of this group because Company B only has an effective 56.25% holding in Company F (75% x 75%). However, Company E and Company F form a separate SDLT group.

9.38 Even if the basic 75% share ownership test is satisfied, two economic ownership tests must also be satisfied in order for an SDLT group to exist.

---

35 See *J Sainsbury Plc v O'Connor* [1991] STC 318.
36 Sch 7, para 1(4).

The first is that the parent must be entitled to at least 75% of the profits of the subsidiary available for distribution to its equity holders. The second economic test is that the parent must be entitled to no less than 75% of the assets of the subsidiary available for distribution to its equity holders on a winding up. Schedule 7, paragraph 1(6) incorporates in large measure the corporation tax group relief tests contained in Schedule 18 to the Income and Corporation Taxes Act 1988, for calculating the relevant income and asset entitlements. These rules are outside the scope of this book, but particular care should be taken in any case where the group has taken out any non-commercial loans.

Restrictions on availability of group relief

9.39 Group relief is not available if, at the effective date of the transaction, various arrangements exist. These provisions are aimed at preventing the relief being available where the intra-group transaction is really aimed at reducing the SDLT charge when the property, or an interest in it, is sold to a non-group person. However, the provisions are very widely drafted with the result that innocent intra-group transactions can be denied relief unless care is taken. There are three restrictions which apply as follows:[37]

1. at the effective date there are arrangements in existence whereby at that time or at a later time a third party has or could obtain control of the purchaser but not of the vendor;

2. the transaction is effected pursuant to an arrangement whereby any part of the consideration for the transaction is to be provided or received directly or indirectly by a non-group member;

---

37 Sch 7, para 2.

3. the transaction is effected pursuant to an arrangement whereby the vendor and the purchaser are to cease to be members of the same group as a result of the purchaser ceasing to be a 75% subsidiary of the vendor or a third company.

9.40 Restrictions **1.** and **3.** above are aimed at preventing group relief being available in cases where the purchaser might or does leave the group holding the property in question following an elimination of SDLT at up to 4% on the property transfer and with instead stamp duty at 0.5% applying on the sale of the purchaser company's shares. Note that under restriction **1.**, it is not a requirement for the purchaser to actually leave the group but simply that there were arrangements in place whereby it might do so. This restriction is widely worded, and an entirely unrelated or prior transaction may cause the relief to fail, for example, an option held by a third party over shares in the purchaser.

Restriction **2.** is widely drafted and the legislation specifically provides that an arrangement will be within **2.** if under it the vendor, purchaser or other group company is to be enabled to provide any of the consideration or is to part with any of it in consequence of any transaction involving a payment or other disposition by a non-group person. Potentially, the restrictions could apply to deny relief where the finance for the intra-group transaction has been provided from a third party lender on arm's length terms. However, in 1998 the Inland Revenue confirmed in a Statement of Practice[38] that this restriction would not generally apply in the case where third party finance is obtained on ordinary commercial terms and where the intra-group transaction was not to be followed by the sale or lease of the property in question to a person outside the group in circumstances where stamp duty would

---

[38] Inland Revenue Statement of Practice SP3/98.

not be paid in the ordinary course. The Inland Revenue has not yet confirmed whether or not this statement is to apply to the position under SDLT, although it is understood that it is being revised for SDLT purposes.

9.41 For purposes of these restrictions the term 'arrangements' is widely defined to include any 'scheme, agreement or understanding, whether or not legally enforceable'.[39]

It is clear that an arrangement will exist in cases which fall short of a binding contract or agreement existing between two parties. However, it would appear that in order for an arrangement to exist there must still be some form of understanding or non-binding agreement in place between two parties. A general intention to dispose of the transferee company at some time in the future, but where no purchaser has been identified, should not generally constitute an arrangement. For the purposes of the similar stamp duty provisions, the term 'arrangement' was not defined although the Inland Revenue sought to place a wide meaning on the term as set out in its Statement of Practice SP3/98. It was felt, however, that existing case law did not necessarily support the approach taken by the Inland Revenue, in particular, its assertion that relief would be denied if there is 'an expectation that a disqualifying event will happen in accordance with the arrangements and no likelihood in practice that it will not'. The concern under SDLT is that the wide statutory definition now given to the term 'arrangements' may enable the Inland Revenue to apply these provisions very widely.

Withdrawal of group relief

9.42 Where group relief has been granted it will be withdrawn if:

---

39 Sch 7, para 2(5).

1. the purchaser ceases to be a member of the same group as the vendor within three years of the transaction, or in pursuance of arrangements made before the end of that three-year period; and

2. at the time that the purchaser leaves the group the purchaser, or a company associated with the purchaser, owns the property or an interest derived from the property,

and there has not been a subsequent intra-group transfer of the property at market value for which group relief was available but was not claimed.[40] In these circumstances the group relief originally granted is 'clawed back' and SDLT must then be paid within 30 days of the purchaser leaving the group, on the basis that the consideration for the prior intra-group transaction was its market value at the effective date of the intra-group transaction.

9.43 It should be noted that these clawback provisions are in addition to the provisions which apply where a lease, on the grant of which group relief was obtained, is assigned to a non-group member. In this case the assignment is treated as if it was the grant of a lease.[41] These provisions are dealt with in **para 4.11**.

9.44 The provisions dealing with the clawback of group relief are closely based on the provisions relating to stamp duty which were introduced by the Finance Acts 2002 and 2003. The provision which applies the clawback in those cases in which the property in question has been transferred by the purchaser to a company associated with the purchaser (typically a subsidiary of the purchaser) were introduced by the Finance Act 2003 to block various planning techniques which

---

40 Sch 7, para 3(1).
41 Sch 17A, para 11.

exploited certain loopholes existing in the original Finance Act 2002 legislation. Whilst the changes are effective to block most of the schemes which were implemented to avoid the application of these provisions, it appears that the legislation has not closed all of the potential loopholes.

Example 1:

Company A owns 100% of Company B which in turn owns 100% of Company C. Company A transfers a freehold property to Company B for nil consideration on 1 April 2004 at a time when the market value of the property is £500,000 and group relief is claimed on the transfer. Company B then transfers the freehold property to Company C for £100,000 on 1 June 2004 and Company C claims group relief on this transfer. Company A then sells the shares in Company B to an unconnected third party on 1 March 2006 and accordingly Company B and Company C leave the group. The market value of the freehold property on that date is £1m. As Company B has left the same group as Company A before the end of three years from the date of the initial intra-group transfer, and its associated company, Company C, owns the property, the group relief is withdrawn and Company B must pay SDLT on the market value of the property on 1 April 2004, namely at 4% of £500,000. However, group relief is not withdrawn on the transfer from Company B to Company C as Companies B and C have themselves remained within the same group.

Example 2:

The facts are the same as those in example 1 save that Company C pays market value for the property it acquires from Company B and pays SDLT on this transfer even though it could have claimed group relief. When Company B and Company C leave the group there is no clawback of group relief claimed by Company B as SDLT has been paid by Company C on a market value transaction involving the property in question.

9.45 Furthermore, it should be noted that if the land interest held by the purchaser (and any relevant associated company) at the time group relief is withdrawn is not the same as the interest which was transferred by the original land transaction (for example, because a lease has been granted to a non-group member out of a freehold interest) then the SDLT payable will be calculated by reference to what the market value of the purchaser's current interest in the property would have been at the date of the prior intra-group transfer.

Example 3:

Company A owns 100% of Company B and Company A transfers a company property to Company B for nil consideration on 1 April 2004 at a time when the market value of the property is £2m and group relief is claimed on the transfer. On 1 October 2004 Company B grants a lease to an unconnected third party for market value. On 1 March 2006 Company A sells its shares in Company B to an unconnected third party and as Company B has left the same group as Company A before the end of three years from the date of the initial intra-group transfer, the group relief is withdrawn and Company B must pay SDLT. However, as Company B now holds the freehold reversion in the property rather than the freehold which was the subject of the transfer from Company A, the SDLT payable is that which would have been payable on the appropriate proportion of the original transaction taking into account the chargeable interest now held by Company B. Thus, if the market value of the freehold reversion now held by Company B would have been £1.8m on 1 April 2004 then the SDLT payable will be 4% of £1.8m, ie £72,000.

Restrictions on withdrawal of group relief

9.46 There are certain cases in which group relief is not withdrawn, even though the purchaser leaves the vendor group within three years of the intra-group transfer or pursuant to arrangements entered into within three years of that date. These are as follows:

1. if the purchaser ceases to be a member of the same group as the vendor because the vendor leaves the group (either as a result of the sale of shares in the vendor or another company in the group);

2. the de-grouping arises as a result of the winding up of the vendor or of another company which is above the vendor in the group structure; or

3. the purchaser ceases to be a member of the same group as the vendor as a result of an acquisition of shares for which relief is claimed under section 75 of the Finance Act 1986 (Acquisitions: reliefs).

Liability on withdrawal of group relief

9.47 Although the purchaser company is responsible for paying any SDLT which is clawed back, if the tax is not paid within six months from the date it becomes payable, then the Inland Revenue may serve a notice on either the vendor company or any company which was a member of the same group as the purchaser at the effective date of the transaction, requiring it to pay the SDLT.[42] In addition, any person who was a 'controlling director' of the purchaser, or a company having control of the purchaser, may be made personally liable for the SDLT. A controlling director is widely defined for these purposes as a director, including a shadow director, who alone or together with their associates controls the company in question.[43] Anyone paying the SDLT has a statutory right of recovery against the purchaser company.[44]

---

42 Sch 7, para 5.
43 The definitions are based on the close company definitions in the Income and Corporations Taxes Act 1988, s 416.
44 Sch 7, para 6(5).

9.48 Whenever one is buying a company which owns a property, it is thus vital to ascertain whether there have been any prior intra-group property transactions to determine whether the clawback provisions might apply and appropriate warranties and indemnities should be sought.

Procedure for claiming group relief and clawback obligations

9.49 Group relief is not automatic and must be claimed by completing Box 9 in the land transaction return with code '12'. The purchaser will need to be certain that the conditions for the relief are all satisfied and in particular that the anti-avoidance provisions are not in point. Supporting documentation, such as registers of members, should be retained. The purchaser can if it wishes choose to pay SDLT by not claiming relief. If relief is clawed back then a return must be made to the Inland Revenue together with the SDLT within 30 days of the disqualifying event taking place.[45]

Reconstruction relief and acquisition relief

9.50 These reliefs largely replicate the stamp duty reliefs contained in sections 75 and 76 of the Finance Act 1986. Whilst they are separate reliefs, each applies in cases where the property being transferred constitutes an 'undertaking' of the vendor company, and the consideration given by the purchaser company comprises or includes an issue of shares.[46] One change from the stamp duty provisions is that the purchaser company does not have to have its registered office in the UK. Reconstruction relief provides a full exemption from SDLT, whereas acquisition relief reduces the charge to 0.5%. In both cases, the relief can be withdrawn in certain circumstances.

---

45 S 81.
46 Part 2, Sch 7.

Reconstruction relief

9.51 Exemption from SDLT is available where one company ('the Acquiring Company') acquires the whole or part of an undertaking of another company ('the Target Company') as part of a scheme for the reconstruction of the Target Company.[47]

9.52 The terms 'undertaking' and 'scheme of reconstruction' are not defined in the legislation and, therefore, take their meaning from case law. Insofar as 'undertaking' is concerned, this means the trade or business of a company and in the context of real property this will generally include not only the trade of developing or dealing in land, but also the holding of property as an investment from which rent is derived. The meaning of 'reconstruction' has been considered in a number of cases.[48] In summary, a reconstruction will exist where all or part of a company's undertaking is transferred as a going concern to another company which is owned by substantially the same persons as the transferor company. A reconstruction will not exist for Schedule 7 purposes if the company's undertaking is being partitioned between two successor companies which are owned by different groups of shareholders.

Conditions

9.53 In order for reconstruction relief to apply, three conditions must be satisfied which are as follows:

1. the consideration for the acquisition must consist of non-redeemable shares issued by the Acquiring Company to all the shareholders of the Target

---

47 Sch 7, para 7.
48 See for example *Brooklands Selangor Holdings Ltd v CIR* [1970] 2 All ER 76; *Baytrust Holdings Ltd v CIR* [1971] 3 All ER 76.

Company. As well as including an issue of shares, the consideration may include, however, the assumption or discharge by the Acquiring Company of all or part of the liabilities of the Target Company;

2. after the acquisition, each shareholder in the Acquiring Company must be a shareholder in the Target Company (and vice versa) and their proportionate holding of shares (although not the exact number) in each company must be the same or as nearly as may be the same;

3. the acquisition must be done for bona fide commercial reasons and must not form part of a scheme or arrangement, the main purpose or one of main purposes of which is the avoidance of tax. 'Tax' for this purpose means SDLT, stamp duty, corporation tax, income tax or capital gains tax only.

Acquisition relief

9.54 This relief is somewhat similar to reconstruction relief in that it applies where the Acquiring Company acquires the whole or part of the undertaking of the Target Company, but it differs in that there is no requirement for there to be a reconstruction, and the conditions are far less onerous than those applying to reconstruction relief. A reduced rate of duty of 0.5% as opposed to a full exemption, applies.[49]

Conditions

9.55 In order for acquisition relief to apply, the following conditions must be satisfied:

---

[49] Sch 7, para 8.

1. The consideration for the acquisition must consist of the issue of non-redeemable shares in the Acquiring Company to either the Target Company or to all or any of its shareholders. (There is thus no need for there to be a mirror shareholding in the Target Company and the Acquiring Company, as with reconstruction relief.) The consideration can consist of, in addition, cash (provided it does not exceed 10% of the nominal value of the shares issued) and/or the assumption or discharge by the Acquiring Company of the Target Company's liabilities.

2. There must not be certain arrangements in place involving the shares which are issued as consideration for the transfer. This provision is aimed at preventing the Target Company or its shareholders effectively 'cashing out' the consideration shares which they have acquired by selling them on to a company or companies connected with the Acquiring Company. Thus the Acquiring Company must not be associated with another company that is a party to arrangements with the Target Company relating to the consideration shares issued.

Withdrawal of reconstruction or acquisition relief

9.56 There are similar provisions to those applying to group relief which can lead to reconstruction relief or acquisition relief being clawed back, and SDLT becoming payable.[50]

9.57 Clawback will apply if the effective control of the Acquiring Company changes within three years of the date of the transaction (or pursuant to arrangements within that period) and at that time the Acquiring Company, or a company associated

---

50 Sch 7, para 9.

with it, owns the property in question or an interest derived from that property. The SDLT payable is on the market value of the property interest at the time of the original transaction, although as with group relief clawback, if the purchaser (or an associated company) owns a different interest in the property at the date of the clawback only a proportion of the SDLT becomes chargeable. Furthermore in the event that the Acquiring Company does not pay the SDLT within six months of the change in control, then the Inland Revenue can require any company that was a member of the Acquiring Company's group at the time of the acquisition or any person who was a controlling director of the Acquiring Company to account for the SDLT.

Restrictions on withdrawal of relief

9.58 There are various exemptions which prevent the clawback charge from applying, which are as follows:

1. control of the Acquiring Company changes as a result of a transaction connected with divorce under paragraph 3 of Schedule 3;[51]

2. where control of the Acquiring Company changes as a result of a variation of dispositions taking effect on death;[52]

3. where control of the Acquiring Company changes as a result of an intra-group transfer which qualifies for relief from stamp duty under the Finance Act 1930, section 42;[53]

4. where control of the Acquiring Company changes as a result of a transfer of shares to another company which qualifies for share acquisition relief under the Finance Act 1986, section 77;[54]

---

[51] Sch 7, para 10(2).
[52] Sch 7, para 10(3).

[53] Sch 7, para 10(4).
[54] Sch 7, para 10(5).

5. where control of the Acquiring Company occurs as a result only of a loan creditor becoming or ceasing to be treated as having control of the Acquiring Company;[55]

9.59 It should be noted that the exceptions set out in **paras 1.** and **2.** above will cease to apply if there is a subsequent non-exempt transfer whereby a company holding shares in the Acquiring Company leaves the same group as the Target Company.[56] For these two exemptions to be withdrawn the change of control of the Acquiring Company must occur within three years of the original land transaction which benefited from the reconstruction relief or acquisition relief, or it must occur under arrangements made within that period. Again, the Acquiring Company or an associated company must continue to hold the property in question or an interest in that property for the clawback to apply.

Claiming reconstruction or acquisitions relief/clawback obligations

9.60 Reconstruction relief and acquisition relief are not automatic and must be claimed by completing Box 9 in the land transaction return. Where reconstruction relief is claimed the appropriate code is '13' and where acquisition relief is claimed the appropriate code is '14'. The Acquiring Company can if it wishes choose to pay SDLT by not claiming relief. If relief is clawed back, then a return must be made to the Inland Revenue within 30 days of the disqualifying event taking place.[57]

---

55 Sch 7, para 10(6).
56 Sch 7, para 11.
57 S 81.

Charities relief

9.61 Relief from SDLT is available to a charity where it purchases an interest in land.[58] Although a relief from stamp duty exists for charities,[59] there are no additional conditions which need to be satisfied apart from the body in question being a charity. The SDLT exemption is, however, subject to various conditions, and furthermore the relief can be clawed back in certain circumstances within three years of the effective date of the transaction.

Conditions

9.62 A charity is defined as a body of persons or a trust established for charitable purposes, a meaning which follows the general law. There is no requirement for the charity to be registered with the Charity Commission. In order for the relief to apply the following two conditions must be met:

1. the purchasing charity must intend to hold the property for 'qualifying charitable purposes'. This is defined to mean that the property must be used in the furtherance of the charitable purposes of the purchasing charity or another charity, or is to be held as an investment, the profits of which are to be applied to the charitable purposes of the purchaser;[60] and
2. the transaction must not have been entered into for the purpose of avoiding SDLT by either the purchasing charity or any other person.

9.63 The Inland Revenue was concerned that charities were being used in commercial property transactions to take advantage of the charities relief

---

58 Sch 8.   **60** Sch 8, para 1(2).
59 Finance Act 1982, s 129.

in the stamp duty legislation. Under the SDLT regime, charities will need to look closely at whether the exemption will be available in those cases where they intend to on-sell a property, because if it could be said that this is part of an arrangement to save SDLT, the relief will not be available, and nor will it be available if the transaction in question cannot be regarded as one which is either in furtherance of charitable objects or which does not satisfy the investment test.

Withdrawal of charities relief

9.64 Furthermore, relief granted will be clawed back if a 'disqualifying event' occurs within three years of the effective date of the transaction or in pursuance of an arrangement made within that period, and at the time of this event the charity holds the property or an interest derived from the property.[61]

9.65 For clawback purposes, a 'disqualifying event' is either of the following:

1. the purchasing charity ceases to be established for charitable purposes only; or
2. the property in question ceases to be used for the charitable purposes of the charity or as an investment.

9.66 In addition, if charities relief has been obtained on the grant of a lease to a charity and the lease is later assigned to a non-charity, the assignment is treated as the grant of a lease.[62] These provisions are dealt with in **para 4.11**.

---

61 Sch 8, para 2(1).
62 Sch 17A, para 11.

Procedure for claiming charities relief and clawback obligations

9.67 Charities relief is not automatic and must be claimed by completing Box 9 in the land transaction return with code '20' and providing the charity's registered number if it has one. The purchasing charity can if it wishes choose to pay SDLT by not claiming the relief. If the relief is clawed back then a return must be made to the Inland Revenue within 30 days of the disqualifying event taking place.[63]

Bodies established for national purposes

9.68 A land transaction is relieved from charge[64] if the purchaser is any of the following bodies:

- the Historic Buildings and Monuments Commission for England;
- the National Endowment for Science, Technology and the Arts;
- the Trustees of the British Museum;
- the Trustees of the National Heritage Memorial Fund; or
- the Trustees of the Natural History Museum.

These bodies are not charities, but their functions in many ways resemble those of charities. This relief is not automatic and must be claimed by completing Box 9 in the land transaction return with code '21'.

Compulsory purchase facilitating development

9.69 This relief is designed to ensure that a developer of property does not suffer

---

63 S 81.
64 S 69.

a double charge to SDLT where it acquires land from the original owner via a local authority exercising compulsory purchase powers.[65] This is because otherwise, in practice, the local authority would pass on to the developer the SDLT cost incurred in acquiring the land from the original owner, and because the purchaser may have to pay SDLT on its purchase from the local authority, a double charge to SDLT could arise.

9.70 In order to secure the relief, it does not matter if the purchase is part of an agreement between the vendor and the third party developer provided the property is acquired by the maker of the compulsory purchase order. Furthermore, the development of the land must be carried out by the third party developer and not by the maker of the compulsory purchase order or the vendor of the property. The term 'development' follows the meaning in the appropriate planning legislation.

9.71 This relief is not automatic and must be claimed by the maker of the compulsory purchase order by completing Box 9 in the land transaction return with code '10'.

Compliance with planning obligations

9.72 This is another relief which is designed to relieve a property developer of a potential double charge to SDLT, and applies where a developer has entered into planning obligations in the course of a development which requires the developer to make a transfer to a public authority.[66] It is common for a planning authority, as a condition of granting planning permission for a development, to require the developer to enter into planning obligations (for example to provide a new road or a school or a clinic). As the developer will generally wish to transfer

---

65 S 60.
66 S 61.

the additional building works to the appropriate public authority once it is complete, if the developer has to acquire the land in question from a third party and then subsequently transfer it to the public authority, an effective double charge to SDLT may arise. This is because, although it would be the public authority as the purchaser which would be liable for the SDLT, the public authority would generally seek reimbursement from the developer for the amount of the SDLT suffered. The relief is thus one claimed by the public authority.

9.73 In order to qualify for the relief, the following conditions must be satisfied:

1. the transfer to the public authority must be one by a developer pursuant to the conditions of a planning obligation;
2. the transfer to the public authority must take place within five years of the planning obligation being entered into; and
3. the purchaser must be a 'public authority'.[67]

9.74 The relief is not automatic and must be claimed by the public authority by completing Box 9 in the land transaction return with code '11'.

Arrangements involving public or educational bodies – Private Finance Initiative

9.75 In order to prevent certain undesirable SDLT consequences in the context of arrangements under the Private Finance Initiative (PFI), regulations were introduced with effect from 19 December 2003[68] which provide certain reliefs.

---

67 The list of public authorities is contained in s 61(3).
68 The Stamp Duty Land Tax (Amendment of Schedule 4 to the Finance Act 2003) Regulations, SI 2003/3293.

9.76 PFI transactions commonly involve a sale or long lease by a public body to an operating company that grants a lease or underlease back to the public body. The operating company will also typically undertake to construct a building (eg a hospital or school) or other facility and to maintain the building over a specified period. In such arrangements, the public body will pay a global fee (commonly referred to as the 'unitary charge') to the operating company which will include both rent under the leaseback and consideration for the works and/or services. Often, the public body will transfer surplus land to the operating company (for no additional consideration) as part of the arrangements. There is clearly the potential for several SDLT charges to arise under these arrangements, including on both the transfer to the operating company and the leaseback (noting that the leaseback would generally be relieved under the sale and leaseback provisions),[69] a potential charge on the value of the works and on the value of the services. The aim of these provisions is to ensure that no aspect of a PFI transaction should give rise to an SDLT charge other than on rent and/or premium paid by the non-qualifying body. In the paragraphs below, the public body will be referred to as the 'qualifying body'.

9.77 If the conditions are fulfilled, the carrying out of works or the provision of services, and any consideration given in money or money's worth by the qualifying authority to the non-qualifying body to carry out those works or services, will not be regarded as rent or other chargeable consideration. The legislation also provides that if the requirements are fulfilled, the market value of the transfer or lease by a qualifying body and the lease or underlease that it receives back from the non-qualifying body is taken to be nil. Also, the market value of any transfer or lease of surplus land by the qualifying body is taken to be nil. The purpose of deeming the market value of these transactions to be nil is to prevent a charge arising to either party by virtue of an exchange of interests.

---

69 S 57A.

9.78 In order to qualify for the reliefs the arrangements must take the following format:[70]

1. a qualifying body transfers, or grants or assigns a lease of, any land ('the transferred land') to a non-qualifying body,

2. in consideration (whether in whole or in part) for that transfer, grant, or assignment, the non-qualifying body grants the qualifying body a lease or underlease of the whole, or substantially the whole, of that land ('the leased-back land');

3. the non-qualifying body undertakes to carry out works or provide services to the qualifying body; and

4. some or all of the consideration given by the qualifying body to the non-qualifying body for the carrying out of those works or the provision of those services is consideration in money.

The arrangements will qualify whether or not the qualifying body also transfers, or grants or assigns a lease of, any other land (surplus land) to the non-qualifying body. A potential problem with the provisions, however, is that the same non-qualifying body must hold the land interests as well as carry out the works or provide the services, whereas it is common in PFI transactions for different members of a group to be involved in these functions. It is anticipated that this point will be dealt with by legislation or concession.

9.79 For the purposes of these provisions, the following are qualifying bodies:

1. public bodies within section 66(4);

---

70 Sch 4, para 17(1).

2. institutions within the further education sector or the higher education sector within the meaning of section 91 of the Further and Higher Education Act 1992;

3. further education corporations within the meaning of section 17 of that Act;

4. higher education corporations within the meaning of section 90 of that Act;

5. persons who undertake to establish and maintain, and carry on, or provide for the carrying on, of an academy within the meaning of section 482 of the Education Act 1996; and

6. in Scotland, institutions funded by the Scottish Further Education Funding Council or the Scottish Higher Education Funding Council.

9.80 The reliefs are not automatic and must be claimed by completing Box 9 in the land transaction return. As no specific code has yet been provided, the 'other relief' code '28' should be used.

Reliefs for certain acquisitions of residential properties

9.81 Schedule 6A introduces a number of reliefs for certain acquisitions of residential property. These are aimed at preventing a double charge to SDLT in cases where a third party facilitates the purchase by an individual of a residential property by acquiring an existing property which the third party will then on-sell.

Part-exchange of residential property

9.82 When a house-building company acquires a dwelling from an individual or individuals in exchange or part-exchange for the transfer or grant of a major interest in a newly constructed dwelling to the individual, the consideration for the old dwelling is deemed to be zero[71] if the following conditions are satisfied:

1. the individual acquiring the new dwelling does so for their only or main residence; and

2. the individual has occupied the old dwelling as their only or main residence at some time in the period of two years ending with the date of the acquisition.

The relief is available only to the extent the land sold in part exchange does not exceed the permitted area. The permitted area is 0.5 hectares and surrounding land required for the reasonable enjoyment of the dwelling. Where the area of land exceeds the permitted area, SDLT will be chargeable in relation to so much of the consideration as is attributable to the excess land over the permitted area.

9.83 For the purposes of the relief, a 'house-building company' is a company that carries on the business of constructing or adapting buildings or parts of buildings for use as dwellings.

9.84 To cater for the situation where the old dwelling is purchased from the individual by a person other than a house-building company, there is an extended form of the relief. Thus, where an old dwelling is acquired by a 'property trader', that acquisition will be exempt where it is made in the course of a business that consists of or includes acquiring dwellings from individuals who acquire new dwellings from home-building companies.[72] A 'property trader' is defined as either a company, a limited liability partnership or a partnership whose members

---

71 Sch 6A, para 1.
72 Sch 6A, para 2.

are all either companies or limited liability partnerships and which carries on the business of buying and selling dwellings. As with the main relief, it is necessary that:

1. the individual occupied the old dwelling as their only or main residence at some time in the period of two years ending with the date of its acquisition; and

2. the individual acquires the new dwelling for their only or main residence.

However, there are the following further requirements. The property trader must not intend:

1. to spend more than the permitted amount on refurbishment of the old dwelling;

2. to grant a lease or licence of the old dwelling; or

3. to permit any of its principals or employees (or persons connected with either) to occupy the old dwelling.

As with the main relief, the relief is subject to the 'permitted area' restrictions. The 'permitted amount' of expenditure on refurbishment is the greater of £10,000 or 5% of the consideration for the dwelling, but subject to a maximum of £20,000. Refurbishment does not include cleaning or works required to meet minimum safety standards.

9.85 A similar relief[73] is available in relation to a property trader acquiring a major interest in a dwelling from the personal representatives of a deceased individual. For the relief to be claimed, it is necessary that the acquisition is made

---

73 Sch 6A, para 3.

in the course of a business that consists of or includes acquiring dwellings from personal representatives of deceased individuals and that the deceased individual occupied the dwelling as their only or main residence at some time in the period of two years ending with the date of their death. Again the property trader must not intend to spend more than the permitted amount on refurbishment, grant a lease or licence of the dwelling or permit its principals or employees to occupy the building.

Chain-breaking companies

9.86 Where the acquisition of a new dwelling is only possible if the individual's existing dwelling is sold, the failure to sell the existing dwelling may hold up not only the acquisition of the new dwelling by, eg, A, but also hold up the sale of B's dwelling to A and B's acquisition from C and so on down the chain. To prevent the delay that can result, a property trader may offer the service of acquiring A's old dwelling for a reduced consideration to allow A's purchase to proceed. To prevent SDLT standing in the way of such arrangements, a relief is given on the acquisition by the property trader.[74]

9.87 In order for the property trader to qualify for the relief, it is necessary that the individual has made arrangements to sell the old dwelling and acquire another and that the arrangements to sell the old dwelling fail. It is also necessary that the acquisition of the old dwelling is made for the purposes of enabling the individual's acquisition of the second dwelling to proceed. The acquisition of the second dwelling must be an acquisition of a major interest in that dwelling. It is further necessary that the acquisition of the old dwelling is made in the course of

---

74 Sch 6A, para 4.

a business that consists of or includes acquiring dwellings from individuals in the requisite chain-breaking circumstances.

9.88 The relief is subject to the other restrictions applicable to acquisitions by property traders, referred to in **para 9.84** above.

Acquisition by employer on relocation of employment

9.89 To prevent SDLT being a disincentive to such arrangements, the legislation provides a relief[75] to an employer when it acquires from an individual a major interest in a dwelling on relocation of employment if certain conditions are met. In order for the relief to be available, it is necessary that:

1. the individual occupied the dwelling as their only or main residence at some time in the period of two years ending with the date of the acquisition;

2. the acquisition is made in connection with a change of residence by the individual resulting from relocation of employment; and

3. the consideration for the acquisition does not exceed the market value of the dwelling.

9.90 As with the reliefs described above in relation to acquisitions by house-builders and property traders, the relief is subject to the permitted area restrictions. The definition of 'relocation of employment' includes not only a change in the place where the employee normally performs their duties but also would cover the situation where the employee is to move in order to take up a new employment or where their duties of employment are altered.

---

75 Sch 6A, para 5.

9.91 The change of residence must be one 'resulting from' the relocation of employment. In order to demonstrate this it is necessary that:

1. the changes are made wholly or mainly to allow the individual to have their residence within a reasonable daily travelling distance of their new place of employment; and

2. their former residence is not within a reasonable daily travelling distance of that place.

The legislation does not define what a reasonable daily travelling distance is, and as yet no Inland Revenue guidance on this has been published. What is reasonable is likely to depend not only on the actual travelling time but also on factors such as the modes of transport available, distance from the place of work, the circumstance of the individual and the nature of the job.

9.92 As with the relief for acquisitions by house-builders, a similar relief[76] is available where the acquisition is by a property trader and not the employer itself. In order for the property trader to benefit from the relief, the acquisition of the existing dwelling must be made in the course of a business of the property trader that consists of or includes acquiring dwellings from individuals in connection with a change of residence resulting from relocation of employment. In addition, there is the restriction that the property trader must not spend more than the permitted amount on refurbishment of the dwelling.

Claiming and withdrawal of reliefs

9.93 The reliefs are not automatic, and must be claimed by completing Box 9

---

76 Sch 6A, para 6.

in the land transaction return with the appropriate code. For part-exchange with a house-building company this is '08' and for relocation of employment this is '09' (in either case this includes acquisitions by property traders). Acquisition by chain-breaking companies does not have a specific code, and thus is covered by the other relief code of '28'. Where the claimant of the relief is a house-building company it must also provide its Construction Industry Scheme number.

9.94 The reliefs applicable to property traders listed below are withdrawn[77] if certain of the necessary requirements prove not to be met:

1. acquisition by a property trader from an individual acquiring a new dwelling;
2. acquisition by a property trader from personal representatives;
3. acquisition by a property trader from an individual where a chain of transactions breaks down; and
4. acquisition by a property trader in the case of relocation of employment.

Any of the above reliefs will be withdrawn if the property trader:

1. spends more than the permitted amount on refurbishment of the dwelling;
2. grants a lease or licence of the dwelling; or
3. permits any of its principals or employees (or any person connected with any of its principals or employees) to occupy the dwelling.

Where any of the above reliefs are withdrawn, there will be an obligation to file further land transaction returns within 30 days after the date on which the first of any of the relevant requirements ceases to be met.

---

77 Sch 6A, para 11.

Certain acquisitions by registered social landlords

9.95 Relief from SDLT is available for a land transaction where the purchaser is a registered social landlord,[78] and one of the following conditions **1.-3.** is met:[79]

1. The registered social landlord is controlled by its tenants. This means that the majority of the board members are tenants occupying properties owned or managed by the registered social landlord. For this purpose a 'board member' is:

   (a) in the case of a company, a director of the company;

   (b) in the case of a body corporate whose affairs are managed by its members, one of those members;

   (c) in the case of a body of trustees, one of those trustees; or

   (d) otherwise, a member of the management committee or other body which is entrusted with the management of the registered social landlord.

2. The vendor is a 'qualifying body'. Qualifying bodies are:

   (a) a registered social landlord;

   (b) a housing action trust established under Part 3 of the Housing Act 1988;

   (c) a principal council within the meaning of the Local Government Act 1972;

   (d) the Common Council of the City of London;

   (e) the Scottish Ministers;

   (f) a council constituted under section 2 of the Local Government etc (Scotland) Act 1994;

---

78 Defined in s 121.
79 S 71.

(g) Scottish Homes;

(h) the Department for Social Development in Northern Ireland; or

(i) the Northern Ireland Housing Executive.

3. The transaction is funded with the assistance of a public subsidy. The transaction does not have to be fully funded with the subsidy. A public subsidy means any grant or other financial assistance:

(a) made or given by way of a distribution under section 25 of the National Lottery etc Act 1983;

(b) under section 18 of the Housing Act 1996 (social housing grants);

(c) under section 126 of the Housing Grants, Construction and Regeneration Act 1996 (financial assistance for regeneration and development);

(d) under section 2 of the Housing (Scotland) Act 1988 (general functions of the Scottish Ministers); or

(e) under Article 33 of the Housing (Northern Ireland) Order 1992.

It is expected that many cases in which the relief will be claimed will involve sales by local authorities to housing associations.

9.96 The relief is not automatic, and must be claimed by completing Box 9 in the land transaction return with code '23'.

Incorporation of limited liability partnerships

9.97 This relief largely re-enacts the relief from stamp duty contained in section 12 of the Limited Liability Partnerships Act 2000 which applies when a partnership converts to a limited liability partnership (LLP). Relief from SDLT is available[80] on the transfer of land to an LLP when the following conditions are satisfied:

1. the effective date of the land transaction is within one year from the date of incorporation of the LLP;

2. the transferor is a partner in a partnership comprised of all the persons who are, or who are to become, members of the LLP or else is the nominee or bare trustee for one or more such partners; and

3. the proportions of interest held by the partners are the same both before and after the transaction or, where different, such differences have not arisen as part of any scheme or arrangement having as its main purpose or one of its main purposes the avoidance of any tax or duty.

9.98 The relief is not automatic and must be claimed by completing Box 9 in the land transaction return with code '17'.

Initial transfer of assets to unit trust scheme

9.99 Relief from SDLT is available[81] on the acquisition of a chargeable interest by a unit trust scheme if:

1. immediately before the acquisition the scheme had no assets nor had issued any units;

2. the only consideration given is the issue of units to the vendor; and

3. immediately after the acquisition the vendor is the only unit holder.

---

80 S 65.
81 S 64A.

9.100 The relief is not automatic and must be claimed by completing box 9 in the land transaction return. As no specific code has yet been provided, the other relief code '28' should be used.

Right-to-buy transactions, shared ownership leases and rent to mortgage/loan transactions

9.101 These reliefs contained in Schedule 9 apply to certain transactions involving public sector housing. The relief for right-to-buy transactions limits the chargeable consideration for the transaction by disapplying the rule on contingent consideration which might otherwise apply. In respect of shared ownership leases, relief is given by affording the tenant the choice of paying SDLT either on the separate parts of the property in question as each is purchased or on what would be payable if the whole property was purchased on the grant of the lease. The reliefs for 'rent to mortgage' and 'rent to loan' transactions limit the amount of chargeable consideration.

Right-to-buy transactions

9.102 Paragraph 1 of Schedule 9 is based upon a similar stamp duty relief[82] and provides that the rules on contingent consideration[83] do not apply and thus the chargeable consideration for the right-to-buy transaction does not include any consideration payable if a contingency was to occur or any consideration which in fact does become payable because the contingency has occurred. There will be one charge to SDLT arising when the property is sold based on the consideration paid at the time of sale.

---

82 Finance Act 1981, s 107 and Finance Act 1984, s 110.
83 S 51, dealt with in **paras 3.24-3.28.**

9.103 A right-to-buy transaction is defined as either a sale of a dwelling at a discount by a 'relevant public sector body'[84] or the sale of a dwelling in pursuance of the pre-served right to buy under the Housing Act 1985 or the Housing (Scotland) Act 1987.

Shared ownership leases

9.104 This relief is based upon a similar stamp duty relief.[85] It provides that where a lease of a dwelling is granted either by a qualifying body listed in paragraph 5 of Schedule 9 (this includes housing associations, local housing authorities and various others) or is granted pursuant to a right to buy under the Housing Act 1985 and certain other conditions are satisfied then the lessee may elect for a one-off SDLT charge to apply on the grant of the lease. The conditions to be satisfied are as follows:

1. the lease must be of a dwelling giving the lessee exclusive use;
2. the lease must provide for the lessee to acquire the reversion;
3. the consideration for the grant of the lease must include both rent and a premium calculated by reference to the market value of the dwelling; and
4. the lease must contain a statement of the market value of the dwelling.

9.105 Where the various conditions are satisfied the lessee may elect for the SDLT payable in respect of the lease to be a one-off charge calculated by reference to the market value of the dwelling. A further consequence of making such an election is that when the reversionary interest in the dwelling is transferred to the lessee, no further SDLT is payable.

---

84 Defined in Sch 9, para 1(3).
85 Finance Act 1980, s 97 and Finance Act 1981, s 108.

9.106 There are further provisions[86] which provide relief in those cases where the freehold is acquired in stages, known as 'staircasing'. If the purchaser enters into an election then SDLT is charged upon the minimum rent stated in the lease plus the premium which is stated in the lease as obtainable on the open market.

Rent to mortgage and rent to loan

9.107 A rent to mortgage transaction is a transfer or lease of a dwelling to a person pursuant to Part 5 of the Housing Act 1985 whereby a person can buy their home by paying part of the price up-front with a mortgage to acquire part of the property and with the right to purchase the landlord's share later. A rent to loan scheme is a similar concept applying in Scotland pursuant to rights under Part 3 of the Housing (Scotland) Act 1987. In both cases, the chargeable consideration for the transaction is the consideration which would have been payable for the property had the purchaser been exercising a right to buy.

Claiming the reliefs

9.108 The reliefs are not automatic and must be claimed by completing Box 9 in the land transaction return with code '22'. Once a purchaser has elected for relief under the right to buy or shared ownership lease provisions, the election is irrevocable and cannot be changed by amendment to the return.

Alternative property finance

9.109 Sections 72 and 73 provide relief from multiple charges to SDLT for two types of alternative finance scheme. The aim is to ensue that the SDLT payable is

---

86 Sch 9, para 4.

the same as that which would have been payable if the property had been purchased using a conventional mortgage product. Relief is available either where land is sold to a financial institution and then leased to an individual, or where the land is sold to a financial institution and then re-sold to an individual. The relief is only available where the financial institution is a bank, building society or a wholly owned subsidiary of either.[87] Furthermore, the other party to the transaction must be an individual, or a group of individuals including a partnership of which all the partners are individuals. Although these reliefs are particularly important for Muslim property purchasers because of the restriction placed on the charging of interest on loans by Sharia law, it should be noted that the exemptions are not specifically restricted to such mortgages, and thus could apply to other sale and leaseback transactions.

Land sold to financial institution and leased to individual

9.110 Example:

Two individuals enter into arrangements with a bank whereby the bank purchases a property for £200,000 and grants them a 25-year lease with an option to have the reversion transferred to them. The terms of the lease are such that, over the 25-year period £500,000 is paid to the bank. At the end of the lease the individuals exercise their right and the freehold reversion is transferred to them.

Three transactions take place under these arrangements and in the absence of relieving provisions SDLT will be charged on the acquisition of the property by the bank, on the grant of the lease to the individuals and on the transfer of the freehold reversion to the

---

87 S 72(7).

individuals. Where the conditions are satisfied no SDLT is chargeable on the grant of the lease and on the eventual transfer of the reversion, and the substantial performance test in section 44 and the option rules in section 46 are disapplied. The result is that the same amount of SDLT is payable as would be the case if a conventional mortgage had been taken out, ie 1% on £200,000 (£2,000).

Land leased by financial institution – conditions

9.111 In order for the relief to apply, arrangements must be entered into between an individual and a financial institution whereby the financial institution:

1. purchases a major interest in the land;
2. grants the individual a lease (or in the case of a leasehold interest, a sublease) out of the major interest which has been purchased; and
3. grants the individual the right to require the transfer of the major interest which has been purchased.

9.112 Relief is not available in those cases where the individual acquires the property as a trustee or nominee of any person or group of persons which includes a company.[88] The lease to the individual is exempt from SDLT provided that SDLT has been paid on the acquisition of the land by the financial institution.[89] The transfer of the property by the financial institution to the individual is exempt from SDLT, provided the financial institution at all times has held the major interest in the property and the lease has been held by the individual.[90]

---

88 S 72(6).
89 S 72(3).
90 S 72(4).

Land sold to financial institution and re-sold to an individual

9.113 Example:

Two individuals enter into arrangements with a bank whereby the bank purchases a property for £200,000 and sells it to them for £500,000. The purchase price is paid to the bank by the individuals in instalments over 25 years. In this example, in the absence of any relieving provisions, there would be two charges to SDLT. If the conditions (see below) are satisfied, the on-sale of property by the financial institution to the individual is exempt from SDLT.[91]

Conditions

9.114 In order for this relief to be available the following conditions must be satisfied:

1. the financial institution must purchase a major interest in the land;
2. the financial institution must sell its interest to the individual; and
3. the individual must grant the financial institution a legal mortgage over the land interest.

Claiming the relief

9.115 In order to claim the relief, a land transaction return must be completed with the code '24' inserted in Box 9.

---

91 S 73(3).

Collective enfranchisement by leaseholders

9.116 Section 74 provides that where leaseholders act together to purchase the freehold of a property then, provided the conditions are satisfied, the rate of SDLT chargeable is determined by dividing the total consideration by the number of flats. The effect of this is that the rate of SDLT paid will be in line with that which would have been due had the leaseholders each bought their share of the freehold separately.

9.117 In order for the relief to apply, the freehold must be purchased by a 'right to enfranchisement company' (RTE company) acting in pursuance of a right of collective enfranchisement on behalf of the owners of two or more flats.

9.118 Example:

An RTE company purchases the freehold of ten flats and the communal areas for £800,000. In the absence of relief, the rate of tax applicable would be 4% and the tax payable would be £32,000. Under the relief, the total consideration payable (£800,000) is divided by the number of flats (ten) giving the fractional proportion of the consideration as £80,000. A rate of 1% applies to such a consideration as it is between £60,000 and £250,000 and this rate of 1% is applied to the total consideration of £800,000, giving an SDLT liability of £8,000 instead of £32,000.

9.119 The relief must be claimed by completing Box 9 of the land transaction return with code '25'.

Crofting community right to buy

9.120 Section 75 applies a similar relief to that given in respect of collective enfranchisement where two or more crofts are being bought under the Land Reform (Scotland) Act 2003. The relief is claimed by completing Box 9 of the land transaction return with code '26'.

Other reliefs

9.121 The Finance Act 2003 provides various other reliefs which for present purposes are likely to be of interest only to certain specific taxpayers. These include the following:

1. demutualisation of a building society;[92]
2. demutualisation of an insurance company;[93]
3. transfer in consequence of reorganisation of parliamentary constituencies;[94] and
4. statutory reorganisation of public bodies.[95]

All of these reliefs need to be claimed by completing Box 9 of the land transaction return with the appropriate code.

---

92 S 64.
93 S 63.
94 S 67.
95 S 66.

10. Continuation of stamp duty for partnerships

10.01 In order to allow time for consultation on an appropriate SDLT regime for partnerships, various transactions involving land and partnerships have been excluded from the SDLT regime. These transactions continue to be subject to stamp duty and will not give rise to an obligation to notify the Inland Revenue on a land transaction return. However, transfers of land by third parties to a partnership are subject to SDLT.

10.02 The following transactions are excluded from SDLT:

1. The transfer of an interest in land into a partnership by a partner or in return for a partnership interest. The transfer of an interest includes the grant or creation of such an interest, the variation of such an interest and the surrender or release of such an interest. These transactions are excluded whether the land is transferred upon formation or whether the partnership already exists.[1]

2. The acquisition of an interest in a partnership.[2]

3. The transfer of an interest in land out of a partnership. The exclusion applies to a transaction by which an interest in land is transferred from a partnership to a person in consideration of their ceasing to be a member of the partnership or reducing their interest in the partnership. A transfer will be deemed to take place whenever an interest in land that was partnership property ceases to be partnership property. Once a partnership dissolves or otherwise ceases to exist, the property will be treated as remaining partnership property until it is distributed.[3]

---

1 Sch 15, para 10.
2 Sch 15, para 11.
3 Sch 15, para 12.

10.03 For the purposes of the exclusion, partnership property means 'an interest or right held by or on behalf of a partnership, or the members of a partnership, for the purposes of the partnership business'.[4]

10.04 Generally speaking, the transfer of a property interest to a partnership by a partner would attract a charge to stamp duty at the rate applying to the property concerned, but this not the case if a person contributes property to a partnership in return for a partnership share. The transfer of an interest in a partnership is liable to stamp duty at the rate applying to the underlying property, but transactions are often structured to eliminate any possible charge to stamp duty, and similarly stamp duty is not generally paid on the distribution of property out of a partnership. In view of the relative ease in avoiding stamp duty in relation to property transactions involving partnerships, the Inland Revenue is keen to bring these transactions within the SDLT framework after the consultation exercise ongoing at the time of writing.

Partnership consultation

10.05 At the time of writing, the Inland Revenue has circulated draft clauses in relation to a future SDLT regime for partnerships. In these draft clauses:

1. the transfer of an interest in land into a partnership (whether or not in return for a partnership interest, and whether in relation to a new or existing partnership);
2. the transfer of a partnership interest; and
3. the transfer of an interest in land out of a partnership,

---

4 Sch 15, para 13.

would all become subject to a charge to SDLT at the rate of tax applying to the property, ie at a maximum of 4%. The transfer of a partnership interest would include any arrangements under which an interest in a partnership is transferred by one partner to another, or under which an existing partner reduces their interest in the partnership when a new partner joins. The charge applying to the transfer of a partnership interest would operate by reference to the gross market value of the interest transferred, ie without any deduction for any debt to which the underlying property is subject, and irrespective of whether the transferee provides a consideration equal to market value or not.

10.06 On transfer of an interest in land out of a partnership, the draft clauses allow for a credit in relation to any SDLT already paid in relation to the acquisition of the property interest by the partnership. As a result, if partner A contributes a property to a partnership (consisting of one other partner with equal sharing ratios) for a consideration of £600,000, the partnership would pay SDLT at 4% and £300,000 would be credited against the consideration upon which SDLT is payable on the distribution of the property to partner B. The draft clauses contain no provision under which group relief could apply on a transfer of land into a partnership where one of the partners is treated as grouped with the vendor. Industry representations are continuing on the content of the draft clauses. As the draft clauses do not contain transitional provisions, it is not yet known to what extent the proposed charges could affect arrangements made before the legislation is finalised and comes into force.

11. TRANSITIONAL ISSUES

Contracts entered into on or before Royal Assent (10 July 2003)

11.01 Land transactions pursuant to contracts or agreements for lease entered into on or before 10 July 2003 are not subject to SDLT, even if the land transaction is substantially performed or completed on or after 1 December 2003 (or after 11 July 2003 in the case of **2.** below).[1] However, if any of the following takes place after 10 July 2003, any land transaction pursuant to such contract with an effective date on or after 1 December 2003 will be subject to SDLT:

1. the contract is varied, or the rights under the contract are assigned;
2. an exercise of an option or right of pre-emption in consequence of which the transaction is effected; or
3. the purchaser under the transaction is a different person from the purchaser under the original contract, due to entry into a further contract.

Contracts entered into after Royal Assent but before implementation (1 December 2003)

11.02 In the case of contracts entered into after 10 July 2003 (the date of Royal Assent) but before 1 December 2003, if the contract is carried into effect by a land transaction with an effective date before 1 December 2003, the land transaction will not be subject to SDLT. However, if the land transaction is substantially performed or completed after 1 December 2003, such transaction will be subject to SDLT.[2] Even if the contract has been assigned, or the purchaser under the land

---

1 Sch 19, para 3.
2 Sch 19, para 4(1).

transaction is a different person from the purchaser under the contract due to an event referred to in the previous paragraph, the substantial performance or completion of the contract before implementation is disregarded.[3]

Special provisions for stampable contracts and agreements for lease

11.03 Since certain contracts and agreements for lease entered into before implementation were subject to stamp duty in their own right, a person who has the benefit of such contracts or an agreement for lease may have chosen or been required to stamp the contract or agreement for lease soon after it was entered into. An example of a contract liable to stamp duty in its own right is one for a consideration of over £10m which was not followed by a duly stamped transfer within 90 days.[4] The stamp duty practice was that once the contract or agreement for lease was completed, if it had already been stamped, the document entered into on completion was credited with the stamp duty already paid on the contract or agreement for lease. The same applies to the completion of a contract or agreement for lease on or after 1 December 2003 pursuant to a pre-1 December 2003 contract or agreement for lease which was duly stamped, and the SDLT due on the transfer or lease is reduced by the amount of stamp duty paid on the contract or agreement for lease.[5] However, no repayment may be obtained if less SDLT is payable on the lease than the stamp duty payable on the agreement for lease.

11.04 In the case of an agreement for lease (but not a sale contract), the alternative procedure under stamp duty was that both the agreement for lease and the lease

---

3 Sch 19, para 4(3).
4 S 115.
5 Sch 19, para 5.

were presented for stamping at the same time. Where an agreement for lease entered into before implementation has not been stamped, and a lease is granted post-implementation pursuant to that agreement, no penalties or interest will be due on the late stamping of the agreement where the choice was made to wait until a land transaction return is delivered in relation to the lease.[6] In order to meet concerns regarding Land Registry priority periods, rather than denoting the lease with the stamp duty paid on the agreement for lease the procedure is that the lease is reported on a land transaction return which will allow an Inland Revenue certificate to be issued and the interest registered at the Land Registry. To satisfy the Stamp Office that the agreement for lease was duly stamped, the agreement for lease can be deposited with the Stamp Office with the Inland Revenue certificate, which will allow the Stamp Office to denote the agreement for lease with the SDLT paid on the lease.[7] Where more stamp duty is due on the agreement for lease than the SDLT due on the lease, it is assumed that stamp duty will need to be paid on the excess and the Inland Revenue certificate would be relied upon by the Stamp Office to denote the agreement for lease in respect of the balance. Where the lease benefited from a relief, the agreement can similarly be denoted with a stamp to indicate that a relief was available on the actual grant.

Substantial performance after implementation date

11.05 Where a contract is entered into before 11 July 2003 which is substantially performed but not completed after the implementation date, and later any of the events in **paras 11.01.1-3** above occurs, the effective date of the transaction will be the date of such event and not the date of substantial performance.[8]

---

6 Sch 19, para 8.
7 Sch 19, para 7A.
8 Sch 19, para 4A.

Subsale issues

11.06 As described in **Chapter 8**, there is no blanket subsale relief in the SDLT legislation. Where A contracts to sell to B, and B contracts to sell to C, the SDLT payable on a sale from A to C will only be reduced to the consideration passing on the B-C contract where both contracts complete at the same time and the A-B contract is not substantially performed earlier than the B-C contract. The question arises as to what happens where these conditions are not met by virtue of the substantial performance of the A-B contract before implementation. On the one hand, it is arguable that since the completion of the B-C contract occurs after implementation, the transfer from A to C is subject to SDLT on the consideration passing under both contracts. However, the legislation,[9] as further clarified by the SDLT Customer Newsletter No 3, states that the substantial performance of the A-B contract is disregarded. This means that the transfer from A-C can be treated as a qualifying subsale when it occurs.

11.07 Example:

On 1 September 2003, A Ltd contracts to sell to B Ltd a parcel of land. This contract is substantially performed on 30 November 2003 by B Ltd paying 90% of the contractual consideration and then on 1 December 2003 B Ltd contracts to sell the land to C Ltd by way of subsale. On 31 January 2004, the contracts are completed by a conveyance from A Ltd to C Ltd. SDLT will only apply to the consideration passing under the contract between B Ltd and C Ltd, even though the first contract was substantially performed before completion. This is because the first contract was substantially performed before implementation.

---

9 Sch 19, para 4(3).

Options

11.08 To prevent avoidance by the grant of options before implementation reducing the taxable consideration on exercise, the legislation contains different transitional provisions applicable to options and rights of pre-emption. The avoidance in question might involve the grant of an option for substantial consideration, where such option is not presented for stamping, with a reduced consideration payable on exercise of the option, which would be after implementation. The legislation states[10] that where an option or right of pre-emption is acquired on or after 17 April 2003, the consideration for the grant of the option or right is included in the consideration taken into account for SDLT purposes on exercise of the option or right after implementation. Where an option or right of pre-emption is granted prior to 17 April 2003, but is varied on or after that date, the same rule would apply.[11]

---

10 Sch 19, para 9(2).
11 Sch 19, para 9(3).

12. COMMON PROPERTY DEVELOPMENT AGREEMENTS

Building leases

12.01 Commercial and residential developers will often enter into arrangements with landowners involving building works. A simple example of such a transaction is where the landowner enters into an agreement for lease with the developer, whereby the developer will be granted a lease once it has built a building on the relevant land.

12.02 The question that building leases of the type discussed in **para 12.01** above give rise to is whether the lease should be subject to SDLT by reference to the value of the building works in addition to the rent payable under it, and if so at what time is the SDLT payable? A preliminary question might be whether the works can properly be regarded as 'consideration' given by the purchaser, as it will often be the purchaser which, primarily, will be benefiting from the lease. However, it may be difficult to argue in most cases that the vendor does not also benefit from the works, and as such it seems likely that it should be viewed as consideration.

12.03 On the assumption that the value of the works is capable of constituting consideration for the building lease, one must then consider whether Schedule 4 paragraph 10 (discussed in **Chapter 7**) provides an exemption.[1] As the works are confined to the land acquired and are not done by the vendor or a connected party of the vendor, the sole question is whether the works are to take place after the effective date of the transaction. Since the purchaser would go into possession of the land under the agreement for lease, this would appear to constitute substantial

---

1 It may also be necessary to consider the issues raised by *Prudential v IRC* [1992] STC 863 mentioned below, which apply, but are less common in, the context of a lease.

performance of the agreement, thereby triggering the effective date of the transaction in relation to the agreement for lease, so that the consideration need not take into account the value of the building works. If this is the case, the obligation to pay SDLT is also triggered at that point, giving rise to the difficulty of calculating SDLT on the rent, as this may be uncertain or unascertained at the time the building works commence. The purchaser/tenant would need to pay by reference to its best estimate of the duty and reassess accordingly once the rent is ascertained (see more specifically **paras 5.33-5.56**). An additional difficulty to note is that the term of the lease, which commences at substantial performance, is also unknown at this point. The approach to be taken in these circumstances is discussed in **para 5.70**.

12.04 There is also a further issue to be aware of in these situations, which is that the lease grant itself constitutes an additional notifiable transaction and here the works would have been carried out before the effective date of that transaction (ie when the lease is granted). Accordingly, whilst credit is available for duty paid on the agreement for lease, further SDLT may be due by reference to the value of the works on lease grant if this can be viewed as consideration on general principles. In conversations with the authors the Inland Revenue has indicated that it would not generally seek SDLT in circumstances where Schedule 4, paragraph 10 would apply at substantial performance of the agreement.

12.05 In light of the above, if it is possible for a building lease of the type described to be granted prior to the works commencing, this would put the application of the exemption in paragraph 10 beyond doubt, as it is then clear that the works have taken place after the effective date of the transaction. However, it is understood that, where the conditions in paragraph 10 are satisfied in relation to the agreement for lease, generally, the Inland Revenue would not seek to bring into account the value of the works in calculating any SDLT due on the grant of the lease.

Forward sales

12.06 In the past, it has been quite common for developers to sell a site to a purchaser (eg a pension fund) on the basis that, at the same time, a second contract would be entered into between the same parties whereby the developer would also agree to build a building and arrange for it to be let to tenants.

12.07 It might be argued that, so long as it is not a condition of the sale contract that the vendor carries out the works (or where this obligation is in a separate building agreement), paragraph 10 avoids any charge on the building works. However, it would appear that the Inland Revenue does not consider that paragraph 10 is attempting to deal with this situation. The works themselves are not, in any event, consideration for the land acquisition by the purchaser. However, the consideration paid for the works might be viewed as consideration for the acquisition of a transaction represented by the acquisition of the finished building. It may well be appropriate to consider Schedule 4, paragraph 4 in this situation, and ask whether the payment by the purchaser for the building works is essentially all part of the same bargain with the acquisition of the building plot.

12.08 Further, it may well be existing guidance relating to stamp duty should also be considered in this context, and in particular the case of *Prudential v IRC*[2] and the subsequent Inland Revenue Statement of Practice.[3] In very general terms, in the light of the Inland Revenue guidance, the practice in relation to stamp duty was to ensure that there were two separate contracts in relation to the land transaction and the building works, and that the contracts were

---

2 [1992] STC 863.
3 SP8/93.

genuinely independent of each other. This was taken to mean that a default on one of the contracts (eg the building works contract) would not render the other contract (eg the land contract) unenforceable. If this practice is followed in future, it should mean that the building works are not part of the same bargain for Schedule 4, paragraph 4 purposes and therefore not consideration for the purposes of paragraph 10 so long as the provisions in SP8/93 are complied with.

12.09 This is one of the many areas which remains unclear,[4] but perhaps the appropriate safe course of action is to both comply with paragraph 10 and the requirements set out in the *Prudential* case (as supplemented by existing Inland Revenue guidance) in order to avoid SDLT being assessable by reference to the value of the building works. Accordingly, the land interest should be transferred pursuant to a separate independent contract, and that contract should not make it a condition that the works are carried out by the vendor or a connected party. Further, the works would be carried out after the land had been transferred pursuant to a separate independent contract.

12.10 These forward sale agreements can also involve further consideration becoming payable to the developer by reference to lettings achieved. Here, it might be possible to attribute such further consideration to the building works, which may not constitute chargeable consideration for the land transaction. If attributable to the land sale, special rules would apply to determine the consideration and a further land transaction return itself would be required once the consideration is ascertained (see **paras 3.30-3.34**).

---

4 At the time of writing, the Inland Revenue was considering the extent to which the existing guidance in relation to *Prudential* would apply for SDLT purposes. There is a possibility that, under revised guidance in the SDLT context, it will be more difficult to show that the construction contract is independent of the land contract.

Use of subsales

12.11 Developers have often relied on stamp duty subsale relief in order to avoid paying stamp duty on site assembly. But how does this apply in the context of SDLT?

12.12 Example:

A landowner contracts to sell a site to a developer. Before the developer completes that contract, it contracts to sell the property to an investor, subject to the developer agreeing to carry out the development of the site. However, unless the contract is completed at the same time as the first contract and the first contract is not substantially performed before the second contract, two charges to SDLT will arise. It is this second requirement relating to substantial performance that would be likely to prevent the relief applying, because the developer would appear to need to go into possession in order to carry out the works, even if arrangements can be made so that the developer does not pay the landowner until the completion of the second contract. Accordingly, both transactions would give rise to separate SDLT charges.

12.13 If the example was varied so that the carrying out of the development works was delayed until after the second contract is completed (simultaneous with the first contract) then only one charge to duty would arise. Furthermore, it may also be possible to avoid an SDLT charge arising on the second transaction by reference to the value of the works carried out by the developer (see above for further details). See also **Chapter 8** for more details on subsales. Alternatively, and subject to security issues, it may be preferable for the developer to avoid a purchase contract altogether and instead carry out development works pursuant to a development agreement providing for a share in the profits of the ultimate sale.

Rent-sharing arrangements

12.14 Joint venture-type arrangements involving a developer can sometimes take the form of rent-sharing arrangements. For example, a landowner might agree to grant a 99-year lease to a developer for a rent to be calculated by reference to a percentage of the rent generated from leases granted by the developer out of the 99-year lease. In addition to the issues outlined above in relation to whether the building works undertaken by the developer constitute consideration for the grant of the lease, there is also the issue of SDLT on the rent payable under the leases to contend with, in particular the administrative burden of filing successive land transaction returns. If the developer enters into possession before the grant of the lease, a land transaction return would be due on that event. A further land transaction return would be due at each anniversary of entry into possession before grant, followed by another return on grant of the lease. As the consideration is uncertain, yet another land transaction return would be due at the end of the fifth year of the lease. These issues are discussed in further detail in **Chapter 5** above.

Agreements with local authorities

12.15 There are various reliefs relating to transactions involving local authorities (see **Chapter 9**) which cover compulsory purchase facilitating development and compliance with planning obligations. However, there does not appear to be any relief in relation to circumstances where a developer is required to carry out works to the infrastructure of an area as part of the consideration for a land transaction. Therefore, it would seem that the market value of such services would need to be taken into account in calculating the consideration for the relevant land transaction.

13. Basic planning possibilities under SDLT

Introduction

13.01 This chapter is concerned with basic planning techniques which may be available to taxpayers to mitigate or eliminate SDLT. It must be appreciated that planning under the SDLT regime will be quite different to planning under the old stamp duty regime. This is because, not only have a number of the old stamp duty loopholes been closed but, more fundamentally, because the new tax is based upon radically difference concepts and principles from those which applied under stamp duty. In particular, SDLT is a tax on land transactions and is a 'compulsory' tax which is enforced by a self-assessment regime. Stamp duty, much of the legislation for which went back to the 19th century, was a 'voluntary' tax on documents, and was underpinned by legal concepts such as whether a transfer or a conveyance on sale had been created. The most secure planning under the SDLT regime is thus likely to concentrate on structuring the transaction in question in a way which takes into account the scope of the legislation and any relevant reliefs and exemptions. As a general matter, taxpayers would be well advised to carry out any planning well ahead of any sale, and ideally well before the property in question has been marketed for sale.

13.02 A further issue under SDLT is the power of the Treasury to make regulations at any time to block avoidance possibilities.[1] As a result, it may be that a transaction structure is chosen, but by the time the transaction is carried out the planning is no longer effective. This contrasts with the position under stamp duty where, generally, a stamp duty planning technique would remain available at least until the next Finance Act.

---

1 S 109.

13.03 There is also the issue as to how the courts are likely to view SDLT planning if a transaction or structure is challenged by the Inland Revenue. There has always been some doubt as to whether the principles of purposive statutory interpretation developed by the courts in a series of cases commencing with *WT Ramsay v IRC*[2] and *Furniss (Inspector of Taxes) v Dawson*[3] and most recently expounded by the House of Lords in *MacNiven v Westmoreland*[4] applied to stamp duty. In *Ingram v IRC*,[5] the High Court held that the *Ramsay* principle could apply to stamp duty, and the recent decision of the Hong Kong Court of Final Appeal in *Collector of Stamp Revenue v Arrowtown Assets Ltd*[6] whilst not binding on UK courts, might be said to support that approach. However, it was still not generally accepted that the *Ramsay* approach did apply to stamp duty, and support for this view was found in Lord Hoffmann's speech in *MacNiven*. However there would appear to be little doubt that the principles of statutory interpretation as laid down in *MacNiven* could apply to a tax such as SDLT, which is charged by reference to transactions and not on documents. The courts are thus likely to take cognisance of all the facts of any particular transaction in order to determine the true nature of the transaction that has taken place when deciding how the SDLT provisions should be applied.

13.04 Whenever any form of planning is being contemplated, the commercial and other tax consequences that may arise must be carefully considered.

Use of exemptions and reliefs

13.05 Obviously, all available exemptions and reliefs should be claimed wherever they are applicable. Most reliefs are not automatic and must be claimed by

---

2 [1982] AC 300.
3 [1984] AC 474.
4 [2001] STC 327.

5 [1986] Ch 585.
6 FACV No 4 of 2003.

completing Box 9 on the land transaction return with the appropriate code. In particular one must always check whether land is within a disadvantaged area because of the total exemption which applies with respect to commercial property and the exemption for residential property where the consideration does not exceed £150,000.

Purchase of existing leases

13.06 The purchase of an existing rack rent lease, whether or not for a premium, will not incur the new lease duty charge, and will give rise to a liability to SDLT on only the consideration (if any) paid for the purchase. However, if the lease in question has previously benefited from certain exemptions on grant, including group relief, charities relief and sale and leaseback relief (see **para 4.11**), the assignment of the lease is deemed to be the grant of a new lease on identical terms to the actual lease and for a term equal to the unexpired portion of the lease. Further, as noted in **para 4.18**, care must be taken if acquiring a lease before the end of its fifth year where the consideration for the grant was contingent, uncertain or unascertained.

Grant shorter leases with options to renew

13.07 One means of deferring some of the SDLT payable would be to grant leases which have shorter initial terms but which provide one (or both) of the parties with an option to renew the lease at the end of its initial period. Whilst this will not result in an overall lower rate of duty if the lease is renewed, it will defer some of the tax payable until the renewal. This route may be preferable to granting a longer lease where the tenant has a break right as, in addition to the cashflow cost, there is no refund of duty in the event that the break right is exercised. However, if SDLT rates have gone up when the lease is renewed, the higher rates will apply, and as the lease granted pursuant to the option will be treated as linked to the first lease, the SDLT payable will be on the basis of the NPV of the aggregate term less the SDLT already paid. This route thus provides at best a deferral of SDLT.

Grant of a lease rather than a freehold

13.08 In certain cases where a purchaser and a vendor are considering the sale and purchase of a freehold interest in a property it may be that, commercially and from a tax perspective, the parties would be equally content with the grant of a long lease under which all (or the bulk of) the consideration takes the form of rent. In this situation, it may be possible to structure matters such that the SDLT payable is at 1% on the NPV of the rents, rather than at 4% on any premium consideration.

Partnerships

13.09 Until the provisions dealing with partnerships and SDLT are introduced (see **Chapter 10**) it may be possible to mitigate an SDLT charge by use of a partnership. Contributions of property into a partnership are currently excluded from the new SDLT regime (ie the old stamp duty regime still applies). Further, it is accepted by the Inland Revenue that no stamp duty liability arises in respect of such a contribution, although some care must be taken in the drafting of the documentation. The partnership should be established and the property contributed to it before the property is marketed. Subsequently, the partnership interests could be sold to a purchaser, together with the shares in the general partner of the partnership. Again, so long as care is taken in documenting the transfer of the partnership interests, no liability to SDLT or stamp duty will arise on the transfer of these interests as the legislation currently stands. The possible application of the *Ramsay* approach to any such transaction would also need to be considered.

Unit trusts

13.10 It may be possible to mitigate SDLT by initially transferring a property to an offshore unit trust in exchange for units issued in that unit trust. There is a specific SDLT exemption contained in section 64A on a property transfer into a unit trust, where the transferor is the only holder of units following the property transfer and the unit trust owns no other assets. The units in the unit trust could then be sold by the holder to a third-party purchaser, and there should be no stamp duty or stamp duty reserve tax charge on that sale if the units are in a non-UK unit trust. Again, any such initial transfer of the property should be done at a suitably early stage. The possible application of the *Ramsay* approach to any such transaction would also need to be considered.

Selling property companies

13.11 The sale of a UK company owning a UK property interest is currently subject to stamp duty at 0.5%, whilst the sale of a non-UK company owning a UK property interest is not generally subject to any stamp duty charge. Until such time (if any) as SDLT is introduced on the sale of property-rich companies, the purchase of a company owning the property, rather than the property itself, remains an attractive way of mitigating or eliminating an SDLT charge. The purchase of a company will raise other tax and commercial issues, which will need to be carefully considered.

13.12 A purchaser of properties should also consider acquiring each new property into a separate company so as to be able to offer a future purchaser the option of acquiring a single purpose company rather than the property. Furthermore, by using group relief, companies can at an early stage plan for possible future disposals of their existing properties by transferring them into single purpose companies. The anti-avoidance provisions applying to group relief and the three-year clawback provisions will need to be carefully considered.

Use of licences

13.13 As licences to occupy land are exempt from SDLT, in certain circumstances the grant of a licence may be a useful way of avoiding an SDLT charge. This is mentioned further in **Chapter 5**.

Apportionment of consideration to chattels

13.14 Where a property purchase includes furniture, chattels and other loose items, it still remains legitimate to apportion a reasonable part of the purchase consideration to the non-property items on which no SDLT (or stamp duty) will be payable. In the case of a sale and purchase of a hotel, it may also be possible to apportion part of the consideration to other assets such as stock and goodwill, which will reduce the SDLT charge. This is particularly useful where the aggregate purchase consideration is around one of the SDLT thresholds of £60,000, £150,000, £250,000 or £500,000. If the item is a fixture and not a chattel, then SDLT will be chargeable on the consideration attributable to it. For an item to be regarded as a fixture it must, as a starting point, be annexed to the property. The question then to be considered is the degree and purpose of annexation, with particular emphasis on the purpose. In Customer Newsletter no 6, the Inland Revenue has given a list of residential property items which will be regarded as chattels. These include all carpets, curtains and blinds, kitchen white goods and light shades and fittings. Items which will normally be regarded as fixtures are fitted kitchens, central heating systems, mounted ovens and alarm systems.

13.15 Taxpayers will need to take great care that the apportionment is reasonable and can be properly supported. Where the price is paid partly for a land transaction and partly for a non-land transaction such as chattels, a 'just and reasonable apportionment' is required under paragraph 4 of Schedule 4. It is likely that the Inland Revenue will be particularly vigilant in cases where the overall consideration is around a threshold figure and a deduction has been made for chattels.

14. Paying and filing requirements

Land transaction returns

14.01 The most significant change which the SDLT regime introduces is the mandatory requirement for a purchaser of a chargeable interest to pay SDLT and submit a land transaction return. This requirement carries with it compliance and record-keeping obligations which are similar to those applying to direct taxes.

14.02 In practical terms, it means that purchasers will need to have compliance strategies in place to deal with the immediate issues arising from the acquisition of chargeable interests as well as the ongoing issues which may emerge. Ideally, a purchaser should nominate a person to take responsibility for SDLT compliance early on. For advisers, the fact that post-acquisition events can alter a purchaser's SDLT liability presents a new challenge. Many advisers may provide both tax and property advice, so it is important to clarify who will deal with SDLT compliance.

14.03 In October 2003, the Law Society of England and Wales published a list of practical issues which solicitors may wish to bear in mind when providing advice.[1]

Duty to deliver a return

14.04 A purchaser's basic obligation is to deliver a land transaction return to the Inland Revenue when acquiring a chargeable interest. While the acquisition of certain interests falls outside of this obligation it is wise to assume, at least initially, that an acquisition requires a land transaction return. It is also important to remember that certain dealings with land interests, such as variations, may also be subject to SDLT.

---

1 Stamp Duty Land Tax Practice Issues, October 2003, The Law Society.

14.05 A land transaction return must be delivered to the Inland Revenue within 30 days of the effective date of the transaction.[2] SDLT must also be self-assessed by the purchaser and paid at the time the return is lodged.[3] Failure to comply with these paying and filing requirements renders the purchaser liable to interest and penalties as discussed in **Chapter 15** below.

Who is required to deliver a return and pay SDLT?

14.06 The obligation to deliver a return and pay SDLT rests on the purchaser.[4] A purchaser is a person acquiring the subject matter of a transaction.[5] A person will not be a purchaser unless it has given consideration for, or is a party to, the transaction.[6] The following table is taken from the SDLT Manual and identifies who a purchaser is for a number of different kinds of transaction.[7]

Table 14A	
Transaction	*Purchaser*
Land transfer	Transferee
Conveyance	Transferee
Assignment	Assignee
Assignation	Assignee
Grant of lease	Lessee or tenant
Surrender of lease	Landlord
Grant of rights including easement, servitude or profit *a prendre*	Person who becomes entitled to the right
Variation	Person whose estate, interest or right is benefited or enlarged
Making or release of a covenant or condition	Person whose estate, interest or right is benefited or enlarged.

---

2 S 76.
3 S 86(1).
4 S 85.
5 S 43(4).
6 S 43(5).
7 Para 7100.

Types of purchaser

14.07 The SDLT code specifies in the case of different kinds of purchasers the person or persons responsible for paying SDLT and lodging returns. In all cases the important point to bear in mind is that the purchaser is required to self-assess the SDLT payable and lodge the appropriate land transaction return(s).

Companies

14.08 The proper officer of a company or another person having authority (express or implied), such as a director, to act on behalf of a company is responsible for ensuring that a company complies with its obligations under the SDLT regime. A company for these purposes is a body corporate or unincorporated association, but excludes a partnership.

14.09 The *proper officer* of a body corporate is the secretary of the company or a person acting as secretary and, for an unincorporated association or body corporate without a secretary, the treasurer or person acting as treasurer. If a company is in liquidation or administration, the proper officer is the liquidator or administrator.

14.10 Tax which is due from an unincorporated association or a body incorporated outside of the UK may be recovered from the proper officer of the company. That said, the proper officer may retain out of money coming into their hands on behalf of the company sufficient funds to pay any SDLT, and is entitled to be indemnified by the company in respect of any liability imposed on them.[8]

---

8 S 100.

Unit trust schemes

14.11 SDLT applies to unit trust schemes (as defined in the Financial Services and Markets Act 2000) as if the trustees were a company and the rights of unit holders were shares in a company, except when applying the deemed market value rule to transactions with connected companies and in relation to obtaining group relief, reconstruction relief or acquisition relief as discussed in **Chapter 9**. For umbrella schemes, each sub-fund of a unit trust is treated as a separate unit trust scheme.[9]

14.12 A limited exemption exists for acquisitions of chargeable interests by unit trust schemes as outlined in **para 9.99**.[10]

14.13 The issue, transfer and surrender of units in a unit trust scheme is not liable to SDLT, and remains subject to stamp duty and stamp duty reserve tax.

Open-ended investment companies (OEICs)

14.14 The Treasury is able to make regulations as appropriate for securing that the SDLT provisions apply to OEICs.[11] The SDLT Manual states that SDLT will apply to OEICs in the same way that it applies to unit trust schemes.[12]

Joint purchasers

14.15 Where a land interest is acquired by two or more purchasers (other than partners or trustees) only one return needs to be lodged, but the obligation

---

9 S 101.
10 S 64A.

11 S 102.
12 Para 31500.

to lodge a return and pay SDLT is a joint one which may be discharged by any of them. It is advisable that joint purchasers agree who will be responsible for lodging a return and how the responsible party will be put in funds to pay SDLT. Joint purchasers are jointly and severally liable for the SDLT payable.[13]

Partnerships

14.16 For the purposes of SDLT, a partnership means a partnership under the Partnership Act 1890, a limited partnership registered under the Limited Partnerships Act 1907 and a limited liability partnership formed under the Limited Liability Partnerships Act 2000 or an entity of a similar nature formed outside of the UK. A partnership is not to be regarded as a unit trust scheme or an OEIC.

14.17 A land transaction entered into for the purposes of a partnership is treated as entered into by or on behalf of the partners, and not by the partnership. The partners at the effective date of the transaction are jointly and severally liable for lodging a return and paying any SDLT.[14]

14.18 A representative partner may act for the other partners in the partnership. A representative partner is one nominated by the majority of partners to act as the representative. Notice of such nomination (or subsequent revocation) should be sent to the partnership's local Stamp Office, and only takes effect on being given to the Inland Revenue.[15]

---

13 S 103.
14 Sch 15, paras 6 and 7.
15 Sch 15, para 8.

14.19 At the time of writing there is no form of notice of nomination, so it is simply a matter of writing to the partnership's local Stamp Office. It is important that a minute of the nomination of the representative partner and proof of posting is also retained if the Inland Revenue ever requires evidence.

14.20 Note that while having a representative partner means that only the representative partner needs to sign the purchaser declaration at Box 71 of the SDLT1 return form, it is still necessary to provide details of all the partners in the SDLT1 and, where there are more than two partners, an SDLT2 return form will need to be completed for the third and subsequent partners. This can be a time-consuming exercise where there are a large number of partners.

14.21 While land transactions between partnerships and third parties are subject to SDLT, some transactions involving partnerships are excluded from SDLT. Transactions which are excluded include transfers of land into a partnership by partners; the acquisition of an interest in a partnership; and the transfer of land out of a partnership to a partner. In all these cases the applicable stamp duty law will still apply.[16] See **Chapter 10** for a more detailed discussion.

14.22 The transfer of a chargeable interest to a limited liability partnership in connection with its incorporation will also be exempt from SDLT in certain circumstances. See **para 9.97** for a more detailed discussion.

Trustees

14.23 The responsibility of a trustee to pay SDLT depends on whether the trust is a bare trust or a settlement.

---

16 Sch 15, para 9.

14.24 *Bare trust* – a bare trust is one in which property is held by a person as trustee for another person who is absolutely entitled as against the trustee and includes a case in which a person holds property as nominee for another. A person will be absolutely entitled as against the trustee where the person has the exclusive right, subject to satisfying any outstanding charge or the like, to direct how the property is dealt with, or to resort to the property for payment of duty, taxes, costs or other outgoings.[17]

14.25 Where a person is a bare trustee, the SDLT code applies as if the chargeable interest was vested in, and the acts of the trustees in relation to it were acts of, the beneficiary.[18] This treatment mirrors that of beneficiaries under bare trusts for Taxation of Chargeable Gains Act 1992 purposes.[19] A beneficiary of a bare trust will, therefore, be the person liable to pay SDLT and to lodge returns.

14.26 *Settlement* – a settlement is defined for SDLT purposes as a trust that is not a bare trust.[20] Where the trustees of a settlement acquire a chargeable interest they are treated as purchasers of both the legal and beneficial interest and will be responsible for the payment of SDLT and the lodging of returns.[21]

14.27 Where a settlement has acquired an interest in land and SDLT is unpaid or penalties and interest are payable, the Inland Revenue can recover these amounts from the trustees. Any of the trustees may be made liable for the whole amount, but no trustee may be made liable for amounts that (broadly speaking) accrued prior to that person becoming a trustee.[22]

---

17 Sch 16, para 1.
18 Sch 16, para 3.
19 Taxation of Chargeable Gains Act 1992, s 60.

20 Sch 16, para 1.
21 Sch 16, para 4.
22 Sch 16, para 5.

14.28 Trustees who have obtained indemnity cover from the trust may wish to make sure that this indemnity extends to SDLT.

Persons acting in a representative capacity

14.29 A person who has the direction, management or control of the property of an incapacitated person is responsible for complying with the SDLT regime and may retain out of money coming into its hands sufficient funds to satisfy any SDLT payment. To the extent that the representative is not reimbursed, it is entitled to be indemnified in respect of a payment.

14.30 The personal representative of a person who has purchased land has a similar obligation to meet that person's SDLT obligations and may deduct any payment made by them out of the assets and effects of the deceased.

14.31 In the case of a parent or guardian of a minor the parent or guardian is responsible for discharging all SDLT obligations that are not discharged by the minor.

14.32 A receiver appointed by a court in the UK is responsible for discharging all SDLT obligations.[23]

Crown application

14.33 SDLT is payable by government departments and public offices. However, the following purchasers are exempt:

---

23 S 106.

Government

- A Minister of the Crown.
- The Scottish Ministers.
- A Northern Ireland department.

Parliament, etc

- The Corporate Officer of the House of Lords.
- The Corporate Officer of the House of Commons.
- The Scottish Parliamentary Corporate Body.
- The Northern Ireland Assembly Commission.
- The National Assembly for Wales.

14.34 Whilst the Crown can be liable to SDLT, it cannot be prosecuted for an offence, nor can the Inland Revenue obtain a warrant to enter premises under its information powers.[24]

Circumstances in which a return must be lodged

14.35 Determining whether a return needs to be lodged in respect of a land transaction is not always straightforward. Purchasers are advised to assume, at least initially, that a dealing in land will require a return and then determine otherwise.

14.36 As detailed in table 14B, there are two general circumstances in which a return or an amended return may be required: in the case of 'notifiable

---

24 S 107.

Table 14B
Circumstances which require the lodgement/amendment of a return

Notifiable transactions

(a) The acquisition of a major interest in land (including a transaction which is substantially per-formed) such as the acquisition of a freehold or leasehold interest for chargeable consideration.

It is important to remember that where a land transaction is substantially performed a further return will be required if the land transaction is completed by a conveyance.

(b) The grant of a lease for a term of seven years or more for chargeable consideration.

(c) The grant of a lease for less than seven years where the chargeable consideration consists of or includes a premium in respect of which SDLT is chargeable at the rate of 1% or higher, or in respect of which SDLT would be chargeable but for a relief.

(d) The grant of a lease for less than seven years where the chargeable consideration consists of or includes rent in respect of which SDLT is chargeable at the rate of 1% or higher, or in respect of which SDLT would be chargeable but for a relief.

(e) The acquisition of a chargeable interest (other than a major interest in land as discussed in (a) above) where SDLT is payable at 1% or higher, or would be but for a relief.

Transactions/dealings after the effective date

(a) Transactions in which certain reliefs are clawed back.

(b) Transactions involving contingent, uncertain or unascertained consideration which ceases to be contingent or becomes certain.

(c) Leases granted for contingent, uncertain or unascertained rent for which a further return is required at the end of year five of the term.

(d) Leases subject to rent review before the end of year five of the term.

(e) Leases with abnormal rent rises after year five of the term.

(f) A substantially performed contract which is completed by a conveyance.

(g) Transactions which are rescinded or annulled. In this case an amended return can be lodged and an application for a refund of SDLT made.

(h) A later transaction which is linked to an earlier transaction, making the earlier transaction subject to or varying the SDLT payable.

transactions' and 'transactions/dealings after the effective date' of a notifiable transaction.

Transactions arising by operation of law or a court order

14.37 A return may need to be lodged where the transaction in question arises as a result of a court order or through operation of law. However, it is expected that in many cases there will be no chargeable consideration in respect of the transaction, so a return will not be necessary, although the purchaser will need to self-certify using a form SDLT60 if it wishes to notify its interest at the Land Registry.

Notifiable transactions[25]

14.38 The following are notifiable transactions for which a land transaction return should be lodged:

The acquisition of a major interest in land unless it is exempt from charge

14.39 In England and Wales a major interest in land,[26] broadly, means any freehold or leasehold estate. Where a transaction which is substantially performed is completed by a conveyance, a further return should be lodged in respect of the conveyance.[27]

14.40 Chapter 9 discusses those transactions which are exempt from charge and for which no return needs to be lodged. Transactions which are exempt from charge include transfers for nil consideration, transfers on death or divorce and the grant of certain leases by registered social landlords. In these cases, in order to register the interest at the Land Registry the purchaser will first need to provide the Land Registry with a self-certificate (discussed in **para 15.18** below).

---

25 S 77.
26 See **para 2.08**, which states that an acquisition includes a surrender, release or variation.
27 See **para 2.29**.

14.41 Although it is not possible to list every circumstance in which the acquisition of a major interest in land would give rise to an obligation to lodge a return, purchasers should lodge a return in the following instances, even if no SDLT is payable:

1. A transfer of a lease or freehold interest for £1 or greater.
2. A transfer of a lease or freehold interest to a company which is connected with the vendor where the market value of the transaction is greater than nil.
3. Any transfer benefiting from a relief from SDLT. The purchaser should claim the relief in the land transaction return.
4. A transfer subject to a mortgage, as the assumption of mortgage obligations is consideration.
5. An exchange of freehold interests.[28]

14.42 Failure to lodge a return, notwithstanding that no SDLT is payable, leaves the purchaser open to filing penalties of up to £200.

The grant of a lease for a term of seven years or more for chargeable consideration

14.43 The grant of a lease for a term of seven years or more will be notifiable, provided that chargeable consideration is given.

14.44 As noted above, in the case of a transfer of a major interest in land, the grant of a lease for a term of seven years or more for £1 would be notifiable, notwithstanding that no SDLT is payable. However, the grant of a lease for nil

---

28 See **Ch 6** for treatment of surrenders and leasebacks and sale and leaseback transactions.

consideration would not be notifiable. As discussed above, care should be taken where a lease is granted for nil consideration to a company which is connected to the vendor.[29]

The grant of a lease for a term of less than seven years where the chargeable consideration consists of or includes a premium in respect of which SDLT is chargeable at the rate of 1% or higher, or in respect of which SDLT would be chargeable but for a relief

14.45 Unlike the grant of a lease for a term of seven years or more, the grant of a lease for less than seven years will not be a notifiable transaction where no SDLT is payable. Care should be taken in the case of a lease which is granted for a premium which is in the nil-rate band where the average annual rent is £600 a year or more, as the nil-rate band for premiums will not apply and SDLT will be payable on the premium at the rate of 1%.

14.46 While the *grant* of a lease for less than seven years (as opposed to an assignment) on which no SDLT is payable may not require a return, a return would be required if this lease was subsequently assigned for chargeable consideration. This underlines the importance of distinguishing between the grant and the assignment of a lease.

14.47 Example:

A grants a lease for a term of six years to B for a premium of £149,000 with only a peppercorn rent payable. B then assigns this lease for a premium of £1 to a third party, C.

---

29 S 53.

No SDLT would be payable on the grant to B, and no return would need to be lodged (although B would need to produce a self-certificate to the Land Registry to register its interest). A return would, however, need to be lodged by C, even though no SDLT is payable as there has been an assignment for chargeable consideration.

14.48 If no SDLT is payable because a relief applies, then a land transaction return will still need to be lodged.

The grant of a lease for a term of less than seven years where the chargeable consideration consists of or includes rent in respect of which SDLT is chargeable at a rate of 1% or higher, or in respect of which SDLT would be chargeable but for a relief

14.49 The grant of a lease for less than seven years will not be a notifiable transaction where the premium payable is within the nil-rate band and the rent payable is also within the nil-rate band for lease duty. Although, as noted above, where the average annual rent payable is greater than £600, the nil-rate band for premiums disappears and SDLT is payable at the rate of 1% on the premium.

14.50 If no SDLT is payable because a relief applies, then a land transaction return will still need to be lodged.

*The acquisition of a chargeable interest (other than a major interest in land as discussed at **para 14.39** above) where SDLT is payable at 1% or higher, or would be but for a relief*

14.51 The obligation to lodge a return extends to chargeable interests which are not major interests in land where SDLT is payable, for example the grant or assignment of an option or right of pre-emption, or the grant or surrender of an easement.

Linked transactions

14.52 Special rules apply to linked transactions.[30] Where a later transaction is entered into which is linked with an earlier transaction, with the effect that the earlier transaction becomes notifiable or SDLT becomes payable in respect of the earlier transaction, then the purchaser must deliver a return and pay the SDLT due within 30 days of the effective date of the later transaction.[31]

14.53 Linked transactions with the same effective date can be reported using a single return form as if all the transactions were a single notifiable transaction. The purchaser can nominate whether it wishes to receive a single Revenue certificate or separate ones for each transaction reported in the return.[32]

Uncertain, contingent or unascertained consideration

14.54 Where contingent, uncertain or unascertained consideration, as discussed in **para 2.44**, is payable and the contingency occurs or the uncertain or unascertained consideration becomes certain or is ascertained, then within 30 days of this occurrence the purchaser should reconsider the transaction to decide whether a further return should be lodged and additional SDLT paid (or a refund claimed).[33] The requirement to reconsider a transaction does not apply to the extent that the

---

30 See **para 2.37** regarding the meaning of linked transactions.
31 S 81A.
32 SI 2003/2837, para 7.
33 S 80.

chargeable consideration consists of annuities.[34] Where the contingent, uncertain or unascertained consideration is rent, different rules apply to those in respect of premium consideration and a revised return may need to be lodged on the occurrence of various events as outlined in **Chapter 5**.

Substantially performed contract completed by conveyance

14.55 Where a contract is substantially performed and then completed by a conveyance, a return will need to be lodged for both the substantially performed contract as well as the conveyance. However, SDLT will only be payable on the conveyance to the extent that there is further chargeable consideration. For example, where the option to tax in respect of VAT is made after the effective date, this appears to be treated as further consideration in respect of the later land transaction on completion.

14.56 At the time of writing, returns in respect of the conveyance should be submitted to the Manchester Stamp Office. If the purchaser fails to lodge a return in respect of the conveyance, not only will it be liable to a filing penalty of up to £200, but it will also be unable to register its land interest at the Land Registry as it will not have received a Revenue certificate.

Withdrawal of relief

14.57 A purchaser is required to lodge a return if relief from SDLT is claimed. A purchaser is also required to lodge a return if certain reliefs are withdrawn. The reliefs which may be withdrawn are group relief, reconstruction or acquisition relief, charities relief or certain reliefs for acquisitions of residential property.[35]

---

34 S 52(7).
35 See Sch 7 and 8.

Chapter 9 discusses these reliefs in more detail, but broadly they may be withdrawn where a disqualifying event occurs. SDLT is a self-assessed tax, so if a disqualifying event occurs, a purchaser will be required to assess the additional SDLT payable and lodge a return within 30 days after the date on which the event occurs.[36]

14.58 Care should be taken when acquiring companies and other entities to which the SDLT charge attaches, as the act of acquisition may precipitate the loss of relief. Appropriate warranties and indemnities should be sought.

14.59 Example:

A transfers a chargeable interest to its wholly owned subsidiary B. The transfer is deemed to take place at market value, but no SDLT is payable because B lodges a return claiming group relief. Within three years of the transfer B, which still holds the chargeable interest, is sold. At this point the Inland Revenue claws back the group relief claimed and so B must lodge a further return and pay SDLT on the transfer which benefitted from group relief at the deemed market value consideration within 30 days of ceasing to be a member of the same group as A.

Time limit for lodging returns and paying SDLT

14.60 A return must be lodged within 30 days of the 'effective date' of a land transaction, and SDLT must be paid at this time (subject to the right of deferral in the case of contingent or uncertain consideration). Failure to

---

36 S 81.

lodge a return within this time leaves a purchaser open to interest and penalty charges.[37]

14.61 Thirty days is not a great deal of time to comply, particularly where the consideration is non-monetary. It is advisable, therefore, to plan ahead by ensuring that valuations of non-monetary consideration have been obtained. Purchasers should note that the Inland Revenue has the power to inspect any property for the purposes of ascertaining its market value and it employs professional valuers.[38] Obtaining correct valuations, therefore, will be an important part of lodging a return.

14.62 The Inland Revenue has acknowledged that, as SDLT is a new tax, practitioners and their clients may make unintended mistakes in the early days of the regime. By way of concession the Inland Revenue has agreed that for a short period it will forego late filing penalties for returns lodged more than 30 days but not more than 40 days after the effective date of the transaction. A formal announcement will be made at least four weeks prior to the ending of this concession.[39]

Return forms

14.63 A purchaser is obliged to lodge a land transaction return in the prescribed form, containing the prescribed information and with a declaration by the purchaser (or each of them) that the return is to the best of its knowledge correct and complete.[40]

---

37 See **Ch 15**.
38 S 94.
39 SDLT Bulletin 6.
40 Sch 10, para 1.

14.64 The return forms can be obtained from the Inland Revenue's orderline[41] or can be completed online by going to the Inland Revenue's website.[42] Registration is required to use the online service. Note that at the time of writing there is no means of submitting returns online.

Submitting a return

14.65 Purchasers must use an SDLT1 return form to notify the Inland Revenue of a land transaction. They may also need to supply an SDLT2, SDLT3 or SDLT4 return form depending on the circumstances of the transaction. As each return is scanned when lodged, it should be completed in black ink (including the purchaser's signature) and submitted unfolded.[43] At the time of writing, it would appear that the information in the returns is being entered manually at the Inland Revenue until its scanning system is fully operational.

14.66 SDLT returns should be sent to the Inland Revenue's processing centre at the following address:[44]

> Inland Revenue (Stamp Taxes/SDLT)
> Comben House
> Farriers Way
> Netherton
> Merseyside, L30 4RN

or

> Rapid Data Capture Centre
> DX 725593
> Bootle 9

---

41 0845 302 1472.
42 www.inlandrevenue.gov.uk/so/online/welcome.html.

43 SI 2003/2387, para 9.
44 See **Appendix** regarding the address where there is a second land transaction on completion. See also **para 14.55**.

14.67 The Revenue has said that purchasers should only send returns to this address and not correspondence, which should be sent to the purchaser's local Stamp Office.

14.68 If a return has been properly completed and tax paid, then the purchaser will be issued with a Revenue certificate SDLT5. This certificate enables the purchaser to register its interest with the Land Registry.

Returns and forms

SDLT1

14.69 The SDLT 1 is the principal return form that must be completed for all land transactions requiring the lodgement of a return. Photocopies of an SDLT1 cannot be used, as each form has a unique reference number and barcode. This reference number should be recorded, as this is how the Inland Revenue tracks returns. Details on how to complete an SDLT1 can be found in the Inland Revenue publication SDLT6[45] and in the **Appendix** to this book.

14.70 A notable feature of the SDLT1 is that it collects information which appears to have no relevance to the calculation of the SDLT liability. It appears that this is being collected for statistical purposes or to share with other government agencies.

SDLT2

14.71 An SDLT2 must be completed where there are more than two purchasers or more than two vendors. In the case of partnerships this means that,

---

45 SDLT6 Land Transaction Return Guidance Notes.

notwithstanding the existence of a representative partner, an SDLT2 form will need to be completed for partners in partnerships with more than two partners.

SDLT3

14.72 An SDLT3 should be completed where additional information is required to identify the property or the transaction involves more than one property for example, where the address of the property does not fit on the SDLT1.

SDLT4

14.73 An SDLT4 may need to be completed where additional details of the transaction are required including where:

- the purchaser is a company;
- the land transaction is part of a business sale agreement;
- a post-transaction ruling has been received in accordance with Code of Practice 10;
- any part of the consideration is contingent or uncertain;
- arrangements have been made with the Inland Revenue to pay the tax by instalments; or
- there are mineral rights reserved.

SDLT8 and 8A

14.74 An SDLT8 is issued by the Inland Revenue when there is insufficient data on the land transaction return for the issue of a Revenue certificate. This may be because information has been omitted, it is illegible or an invalid entry has been made, for example a letter entered where a number should be.

14.75 The completed SDLT8 should be returned to the Stamp Office address shown on it. If the completed SDLT8 is not received after ten working days, a reminder (SDLT8A), is issued automatically. The SDLT8A states that a land certificate will not be issued until the outstanding information is received.[46]

14.76 Note that the Inland Revenue has acknowledged that, as SDLT is a new tax, practitioners and their clients may make unintended mistakes in the early days of SDLT. By concession the Inland Revenue has agreed that for a short period it will look to process returns and issue Revenue certificates even if returns have been completed unsatisfactorily and contain errors and omissions, although returns containing critical errors will not receive a certificate.[47]

14.77 Other forms:

SDLT5   Certificate – confirming that the transaction has been notified and that the Land Registry may proceed with registration

SDLT6   Guidance – guidelines for completing forms SDLT1, 2, 3 and 4

SDLT7   Standard letter – response to purchaser inquiry

SDLT9 and 9A   Standard letter – potential overpayment of tax and reminder

SDLT10   Standard letter – confirmation that repayment will follow

SDLT12 and 12A Standard letter – further tax/penalty/interest due and reminder

---

46 SDLT Manual, para 60220.
47 SDLT Bulletin 6.

SDLT14   Standard letter – inform purchaser that no further reminders and no certificate will be issued

SDLT15 and 15A Standard letter – potential overpayment of tax due to availability of relief and reminder

SDLT38   SDLT refund authorisation form[48]

Signing a return

14.78 A purchaser, or each purchaser where there is more than one, must sign the declaration on the SDLT1 that the return is to the best of its knowledge correct and complete. This means that a purchaser may not avoid responsibility for an incorrect return by asserting that it was completed by an agent such as a solicitor or accountant. The following table outlines who is required to make the declaration:

Table 15A	
Purchaser	*Person required to make declaration*
Single purchaser	The single purchaser
Joint purchasers	Each purchaser
Partners in a partnership	Each partner or the representative partner (see **para 14.18**)
Trust	In the case of a trust (other than a bare trust/nominee) any one trustee can sign
Company	Proper officer or any other person having authority to act on the company's behalf
Purchasers unable to control their own affairs	The personal representative, parent or guardian, a receiver appointed by a court or the person having the management, direction or control of the property of an incapacitated person (as appropriate)

---

48 SDLT Manual, para 60500.

Power of attorney

14.79 Note that a person may only sign on behalf of a purchaser if empowered by a power of attorney.[49] A person signing with the authority of a power of attorney should write 'Power of Attorney' underneath their signature.

Amendment or correction of a return

14.80 A purchaser may amend a return within 12 months of the filing date.[50] Where the amendment takes place while an enquiry is in progress, the amendment may not take effect until after the enquiry is concluded.[51] Where an amendment is made during an enquiry, the Inland Revenue has stated in respect of similar provisions under the Taxes Management Act 1970 that it is entitled to impose penalties where a return has been fraudulently or negligently made, notwithstanding the amendment.[52]

14.81 The Inland Revenue may amend a return so as to correct obvious errors or omissions within nine months of the date on which the return was delivered or, in the case of an amendment by the purchaser, within nine months of the amendment.[53] It should be borne in mind that an Inland Revenue correction does not involve any judgment as to the veracity of the information in the return. If the Inland Revenue wishes to check whether the information in a return is correct then it can launch an enquiry.

---

49 S 81B.
50 Sch 10, para 6.
51 Sch 10, para 18.
52 Inland Revenue Interpretation 195.
53 Sch 10, para 7.

Loss or destruction of a return[54]

14.82 Where a return or document has been delivered to the Inland Revenue and has been lost, destroyed, defaced or damaged so that it is illegible or otherwise useless, then the Inland Revenue may treat it as not having been delivered. To mitigate the harshness of this provision, the Inland Revenue states that no penalties will be imposed where it has lost the return.[55] It is advisable, therefore, to send all returns by recorded delivery and to retain proof of delivery so that there is no argument about whether the return was actually sent to the Inland Revenue.

14.83 A taxpayer who proves to the General or Special Commissioners that SDLT was in fact paid in respect of a transaction for which a return has been lost or damaged will be entitled to relief from the Inland Revenue demand for payment of SDLT to the extent of the payment.[56] It is important, therefore, to retain evidence of payment.

Failure to lodge a return

14.84 Where a purchaser fails to lodge a return by the filing date (generally within 30 days of the effective date) the Inland Revenue may issue a notice to the purchaser requiring the delivery of a return. If the purchaser fails to comply, the Inland Revenue may apply to the Special or General Commissioners for an order imposing a daily penalty not exceeding £60.[57] The purchaser may also be liable to interest and penalties as discussed in **Chapter 15** below.

---

54 S 82.
55 Inland Revenue response to *Stamp Duty Land Tax Questions from Practitioners,*
published January 2004, PLC Property Law.
56 S 82(4).
57 Sch 10, para 5.

14.85 In addition to the power to demand a return, the Inland Revenue has six years from the effective date of the transaction to issue a notice of determination (a Revenue determination) estimating the SDLT payable and requiring the purchaser to pay this SDLT.[57]

14.86 The Inland Revenue also has extensive powers to conduct enquiries into returns and to obtain information in addition to the power to issue a determination. These are discussed in **paras 15.31-15.70**.

Payment of SDLT

14.87 The responsibility to pay SDLT rests on the purchaser.[58] No contractual term to the contrary can override this.

14.88 SDLT must be paid at the same time that a return is lodged,[59] which must be within 30 days of the effective date. If a return is amended within 30 days of the effective date, then SDLT is still payable within 30 days of the effective date. If a return is amended more than 30 days after the effective date, then any extra SDLT arising from the amendment is payable immediately.[60]

14.89 Note that this payment rule is subject to the right of the purchaser to defer payment (in certain circumstances) in respect of contingent or uncertain consideration or where an appeal is pending.[61]

14.90 Where SDLT is payable because of the withdrawal of a relief, then it must be

---

57 Sch 10, para 25.
58 S 85.
59 One may not be submitted before the other.
60 S 86.
61 S 86(5).

paid at the same time the return is lodged.[62] The return must be lodged within 30 days after the date on which the disqualifying event occurred that gave rise to the loss of relief.[63]

14.91 Where SDLT is payable in accordance with an assessment or determination by the Inland Revenue, it must be paid within 30 days after the assessment or determination.[64]

Payment methods

14.92 The details for payment can be found in the SDLT1 return form. Where large sums are being paid, it is advisable to use direct payment as the presumption is that lost returns and cheques are the fault of the purchaser and not the Inland Revenue.

14.93 Payment options include the following:

Cheque

14.94 Where payment is made by cheque, and the cheque is paid on first presentation to the banker on whom it is drawn, the payment is treated as being made on the day on which the Inland Revenue receives the cheque.[65] The cheque should be made payable to the 'Inland Revenue Only' and sent to the address in **para 14.66** together with the payslip in the SDLT1. Do not fold the cheque or return form.

---

62 S 86(2).
63 S 81.

64 S 86(4).
65 S 92.

Direct payment

14.95 The Internet, telephone, BACS Direct Credit or CHAPS may be used. The information required to do this is:

- payment account;
- sort code 10-50-41;
- account number 23456000;
- the reference number shown on the payslip on page 7 of the SDLT1.

Bank

14.96 A cheque may be paid to the Inland Revenue at the purchaser's bank. The payslip on page 7 of the SDLT1 return form should also be provided.

Post Office

14.97 A cheque should be made payable to 'Post Office Limited'. The payslip on page 7 of the SDLT1 return form should also be provided.

Alliance & Leicester

14.98 If the purchaser has an account with Alliance & Leicester, the completed payslip may be sent to Alliance & Leicester, Bootle, Merseyside GIR 0AA.

Deferring payment of SDLT – contingent or uncertain consideration

14.99 A purchaser may apply in writing to the Inland Revenue to defer payment of SDLT where the chargeable consideration at the effective date is contingent or uncertain and falls to be paid on one or more future dates, of which at least one is more than six months after the effective date of the transaction.[66]

14.100 The deferral does not affect the purchaser's obligation to lodge a return within 30 days of the effective date of the transaction and only applies to uncertain or contingent consideration.

14.101 Deferral does not apply to consideration which is uncertain because the amount is ascertainable but not yet ascertained, for example where the amount of chargeable consideration depends on profits for an accounting period which finishes prior to the effective date. In this case, a reasonable estimate should be made at the effective date and an amendment made to a return if necessary when the final consideration is ascertained.[67]

14.102 No application for deferral can be made in the case of rent or annuities.[68]

Application to defer payment of SDLT

14.103 An application to defer SDLT should be made in writing on or before the last day of the period within which the return relating to the transaction in question must be delivered.[69] In most cases this means that an application must be made within 30 days of the effective date. The application should set out:

* details of the transaction and why it meets the deferral criteria;

---

66 S 90(1).
67 SDLT Manual, para 50900.
68 Ss 52(7) and 90(7).
69 SI 2003/2837, para 11. See the Administration Regulations on the CD-Rom

- the consideration to which it relates;
- the circumstances in which consideration is contingent or uncertain; and
- relevant events when the consideration will cease to be contingent or become certain.[70]

14.104 The Inland Revenue can require further information for the purpose of determining whether to accept an application. The purchaser must be given at least 30 days to comply with a request for further information.[71] If the information is not provided in the time allowed, the Inland Revenue may refuse the application.

Refusing an application

14.105 The Inland Revenue can refuse an application where:

- it is not in the required form;
- it is incomplete;
- further information required by the Inland Revenue is not provided; or
- there are tax-avoidance arrangements where the main object or one of the main objects of the arrangements is to avoid tax or defer payment of tax.[72]

14.106 If an application is refused, a notice must set out the grounds for the refusal and the amount of tax which is due and payable within 30 days from the notice of refusal.[73] Interest on payment will run from the original payment date.

14.107 The purchaser can appeal to the General or Special Commissioners against a refusal by the Inland Revenue to accept an application within 30 days

---

70 SI 2003/2837, para 12.
71 SI 2003/2837, para 14.
72 SI 2003/2837, paras 17-18.
73 SI 2003/2837, para 16.

after the date on which the notice of the decision to refuse the application was issued, specifying the grounds of appeal.[74] The purchaser can also ask the Inland Revenue or the Commissioners to postpone the obligation to pay SDLT pending the appeal.[75]

Accepting an application

14.108 If the application to defer payment of tax is accepted, the notice of acceptance will set out the terms of acceptance and specify the amount of tax payable in connection with the initial return, the dates of relevant events and how tax is to be calculated on those dates.[76] A return should be lodged within 30 days of a relevant event, together with the payment of any SDLT due.[77]

14.109 An application will cease to have any effect if the facts and circumstances relevant to it materially change, if the application contains false or misleading information or if there is a failure to disclose any facts or circumstances.[78]

Deferral – carrying out of works of construction, improvement, repair or provision of services

14.110 An application for deferral of SDLT may be made in respect of the provision of chargeable consideration consisting of works of construction, improvement, repair or services. The application should contain a scheme for payment which must include:

---

74 SI 2003/2837, paras 19-20.
75 SI 2003/2837, paras 22-23.
76 SI 2003/2837, para 16.
77 SI 2003/2837, para 24.
78 SI 2003/2837, para 28.

1. If the works or services are expected to take less than six months to complete, the purchaser must pay the SDLT in respect of that part of the consideration no later than 30 days after the works or services are complete.

2. If the works or services are expected to take longer than six months, the application must set out a scheme of payment of tax at intervals of not more than six months with a final payment to be made 30 days after the works are completed. Payment will be based on the value of the works or services carried out at each stage.[79]

14.111 Towards the end of a period of works and services, the purchaser can apply to the Inland Revenue for the payment schedule to be varied. This is to deal with the situation where the works or services are almost completed but a six-monthly payment is due.[80]

---

79 SI 2003/2837, para 13.
80 SDLT Manual, para 50920.

15. Inland revenue powers

Interest and penalties

Interest on SDLT

15.01 Interest is payable on unpaid tax from the end of the period 30 days after the relevant date until the tax is paid.[1] The relevant date is:

- where group relief, charities relief, reconstruction or acquisition relief or relief for certain acquisitions of residential property is withdrawn, the date of the disqualifying event which meant the loss of relief;
- in the case of an amount payable under an earlier transaction because of the effect of a later linked transaction, the effective date of the later transaction;
- in the case of an amount payable under a lease that continues after a fixed term or leases of an indefinite term, the day on which the lease becomes treated as being for a longer fixed term;
- in the case of a deferred payment of contingent, or uncertain consideration, the date when the deferred payment is due;
- and, in any other case, the effective date of the transaction.

15.02 To reduce the interest payable a purchaser may wish to make a payment to the Inland Revenue on account of SDLT.[2]

Interest on penalties

15.03 Interest is payable on outstanding penalties.[3]

---

1 S 87.
2 S 87(6).

3 S 88.

Interest on repayments

15.04 Interest is payable on any tax which is repaid by the Inland Revenue or on any repayment of a penalty or on any repayment of an amount of SDLT paid on account by the purchaser. Interest is calculated from the time the tax or penalty was paid or the payment of SDLT on account was made. Any interest received is not income of the purchaser for any tax purposes.[4]

Rates of interest

15.05 The rates of interest are those imposed under the Finance Act 1989, section 178.[5]

Penalties

15.06 The SDLT code provides for a range of penalties. The most common penalties which purchasers are likely to encounter are the flat-rate penalty for late filing of a return and the tax-related penalty for late payment of SDLT. Table 15A summarises the more important penalties.

15.07 Example of a flat-rate penalty:

A major interest in land is transferred for £1, but no return is lodged by the filing date. Although no SDLT is payable, a return still needs to be lodged as it is a notifiable transaction. A flat-rate penalty of £100 will be imposed if the return is delivered within three months of the filing date, rising to £200 for a failure to lodge a return after three months.[6]

---

4 S 89(1).
5 S 87(7). At the time of writing the interest rate payable on unpaid SDLT is 6.5%.
6 Sch 10, para 3.

Table 17A

Summary of penalties

Offence	Penalty
Late payment and/or late filing[7]	*Flat rate*: £100 if return delivered within three months of filing date; £200 in any other case *Tax-related*: Amount not exceeding the amount of SDLT payable if return is not filed within 12 months of the filing date
Failure to comply with an Inland Revenue notice to deliver a return[8]	The Inland Revenue can apply to the Commissioners for a penalty of up to £60 per day
Fraudulent or negligent delivery of an incorrect return/unreasonable delay in notifying the Inland Revenue of an incorrect return[9]	Tax-related penalty of an amount not exceeding the difference between the SDLT chargeable and the SDLT that would have been chargeable based on the return delivered
Failure to maintain records in relation to a return or self-certificate[10]	Penalty not exceeding £3,000
Failure to produce documents to the Inland Revenue for the purpose of enquiry into a return or self-certificate[11]	£50 penalty and a further £30 penalty (if determined by the Inland Revenue) or £150 (if determined by a court) for each day the failure continues
Fraudulent or negligent giving of a self-certificate /unreasonable delay in advising the Inland Revenue that a self-certificate should not have been produced in relation to a transaction[12]	Tax-related penalty of an amount not exceeding the amount of SDLT payable
Fraudulent evasion of tax[13]	*Summary conviction:* up to six months' imprisonment or fine not exceeding the statutory maximum or both. *Indictment:* up to seven years' imprisonment or a fine or both

Table 17A (cont)

Offence	Penalty
Assisting or inducing the preparation of an incorrect return[14]	Penalty not exceeding £3,000
Failure to deliver document or to provide information, or make a document available for inspection in accordance with the information powers exercisable by an officer of the Inland Revenue[15]	Penalty not exceeding £300 with a further penalty of £60 a day if the failure continues
A person who is required to comply with a notice issued by an officer of the Inland Revenue under its information powers and who fraudulently or negligently delivers or provides any incorrect document or information[16]	Penalty not exceeding £3,000
Falsifying, concealing or destroying specified documents requested under the Inland Revenue's information powers[17]	*Summary conviction:* fine not exceeding the statutory maximum *Indictment:* up to two years' imprisonment or a fine or both
Wilful delay or obstruction of an officer seeking to inspect property for the purposes of ascertaining its market value[18]	*Summary conviction:* fine not to exceed level 1 on the standard scale

7 Sch 10, paras 3 and 4.
8 Sch 10, para 5.
9 Sch 10, para 8.
10 Sch 10, para 11 and Sch 11, para 6.
11 Sch 10, para 16 and Sch 11, para 11,
12 Sch 11, para 3.
13 S 95.
14 S 96.
15 Ss 93(3) and 93(4).
16 S 93(6).
17 Sch 13, part 8.
18 S 94.

Penalty for assisting in the preparation of incorrect return

15.08 Tax advisers should take particular note of the penalty of up to £3,000 for assisting in or inducing the preparation or delivery of an incorrect return, information or other document that they know is incorrect and is likely to be used for any purpose connected with SDLT.[19]

15.09 If a tax adviser has provided correct information they may still be liable if a return is incorrect and they know this is the case (for example, if a tax adviser is aware that a purchaser has included incorrect information in parts of the return left blank by the adviser).

Liability to pay penalties

15.10 Except where stated otherwise, the purchaser is liable to pay a penalty. In the case of partners in a partnership and joint purchasers, the liability is joint and several.[20] As discussed in **para 14.27** a trustee can be liable to pay a penalty.

Due date to pay penalties

15.11 A penalty becomes due and payable 30 days after the date of issue of the penalty notice.[21] Where a return is amended with the result that more tax is payable, the Inland Revenue has indicated that, unless a purchaser is negligent, it will not automatically impose a penalty.[22]

---

19 S 94.
20 Sch 15, para 7.
21 Sch 14, para 2(4).
22 Inland Revenue response to *Stamp Duty Land Tax Questions from Practitioners,* published January 2004, PLC Property Law.

15.12 The purchaser can appeal against a penalty notice but must do so within 30 days of the date of the issue of the notice.[23]

Inland Revenue's power to adjust penalties

15.13 The Board of Inland Revenue may at its discretion mitigate any penalty.[24] In calculating a penalty the Inland Revenue will take into account:

- the extent to which the purchaser makes voluntary disclosure;
- the extent to which the purchaser provides assistance; and
- the seriousness of the errors or omissions.[25]

No deduction against income, profits or losses for any tax purposes is allowed for a payment of interest or penalties on SDLT.[26]

Land registration

15.14 One of the rationales for introducing SDLT was to bring stamp duty legislation into line with electronic conveyancing. Although electronic conveyancing has not yet been implemented, the registration of a land interest in most cases can only proceed after a return has been lodged. The SDLT code provides that in order to register a land transaction or otherwise reflect it in the Land Register, a certificate of compliance with the SDLT code needs to be produced by a purchaser.[27] There are two kinds of certificate:

---

23 Sch 14, para 5(2).
24 S 99.
25 *Working Together*, issue 15 p 5, Inland Revenue.
26 S 827(1F) Income and Corporation Taxes Act 1988.
27 S 79.

1.   Revenue certificate – SDLT5; or

2.   self-certificate – SDLT60

Revenue certificate – SDLT5

15.15 An SDLT5 is given to the purchaser by the Inland Revenue when a return has been delivered in the prescribed form and SDLT paid. The purchaser must then produce this to the Land Registry to register a chargeable interest.

15.16 The Revenue certificate should contain the following items of information:

- land title number;
- the National Land and Property Gazetteer Unique Property Reference Number;
- a description of the transaction;
- the effective date of the transaction; and
- purchaser and vendor names. [28]

15.17 In circumstances where more than one land transaction is reported in a return, the Inland Revenue will issue a single Revenue certificate unless the purchaser requests separate certificates in respect of each transaction by marking the appropriate box on the SDLT1 return form. [29]

15.18 If the Inland Revenue is satisfied that a Revenue certificate has been lost or destroyed, then it may issue a duplicate. [30]

---

28 SI 2837/2003, paras 4 and 5.
29 SI 2837/2003, para 7.
30 SI 2837/2003, para 6.

Self-certificate – SDLT60

15.19 This is a certificate made by the purchaser that no return is required. The self-certificate must be presented to the Land Registry when seeking to register or note an interest on the Land Register.

15.20 The self-certificate must be in writing in the prescribed form, contain the prescribed information and a declaration by the purchaser (or each of them) that the certificate is to the best of its knowledge correct and complete.[31] The legislation provides that there may be different kinds of self-certificates, although at the time of writing the only form is the SDLT60, which can be obtained from the Inland Revenue.

15.21 Self-certification may be appropriate where the transaction is:

- a freehold or leasehold transfer/conveyance for no chargeable consideration;
- a grant of a lease for less than seven years and both premium and rent do not attract SDLT (see **para 5.68** for a more in-depth discussion) unless a relief applies, in which case a return must be lodged; or
- other land transactions (eg grant of an easement) where no SDLT is payable unless a relief applies, in which case a return must be lodged.

15.22 It follows, therefore, that if no return is required to be lodged and the purchaser does not want its interest notified on the Land Register (for example because it has an unregisterable interest such as a lease of less than seven years), that there is no need to complete an SDLT60 self-certificate.

---

31 Sch 11, para 2 and SI 2837/2003, para 8.

15.23 A person who fraudulently or negligently gives a self-certificate in respect of a chargeable transaction, or who discovers that a transaction in respect of which a self-certificate was given is in fact a chargeable transaction, and who does not remedy the error without unreasonable delay, is liable to a tax-related penalty as discussed.[32]

Land Registry practice

15.24 Although the SDLT regime provides that, except in very limited circumstances, no interest can be registered unless a Revenue certificate or self-certificate is produced, in practice the Land Registry will accept an application if it is sent in without a certificate, provided that there is a statement accompanying the application that a return has been lodged with the Inland Revenue and that more than 20 working days have passed since completion. The transfer should be sent in with the application. In this way the purchaser's priority will be preserved.[33]

15.25 In certain limited circumstances a transaction is excluded from the SDLT code, for example certain transactions involving partnerships.[34] In these cases, it would appear that no certificate of any kind should be required to register a chargeable interest with the Land Registry. It is likely that, as the Land Registry will expect a certificate, a purchaser will need to explain why no certificate is required.

---

32 Sch 11, para 3.
33 Land Registry Practice Bulletin 8, October 2003.
34 Sch 15, para 9.

Record keeping

Land transaction returns[35]

15.26 The record-keeping requirements of SDLT are similar to those which apply for direct tax purposes under the Taxes Management Act 1970. A purchaser who is required to lodge a return must keep and preserve such records as may be needed to enable it to deliver a correct and complete return. The records must be preserved for six years from the effective date of the transaction, and until any later date on which an enquiry into a return is completed or the Inland Revenue no longer has any power to make an enquiry.

15.27 The kinds of records which must be retained include:[36]

- contract/agreement for sale and related side papers;
- details of apportionment of consideration between the land acquired and other assets such as chattels;
- professional valuations obtained;
- plans, maps;
- partnership agreements;
- completion documents;
- records of payments, receipts and financial arrangements;
- deeds of attorney; and
- papers supporting the claiming of any relief.

15.28 The purchaser has the option of preserving these original documents or the information contained in them.

---

35 Sch 10, part 2.   **36** *Working Together*, issue 15, p 5 Inland Revenue.

15.29 The penalty for failing to preserve and keep records is an amount not exceeding £3,000. The Inland Revenue has clarified that this penalty can be imposed for each failure to keep or preserve adequate records in respect of a return. The Inland Revenue has also said that penalties will most likely only be sought in more serious cases where, for example, records are destroyed or there has been a history of serious record-keeping failure.[37]

Self-certificates[38]

15.30 The requirement to keep and preserve records in respect of self-certificates mirrors that in respect of land transaction returns.

Compliance

15.31 The Inland Revenue has a range of different powers at its disposal to monitor and promote compliance. The following paragraphs deal with the Inland Revenue's powers to enquire into returns, to issue assessments and to require information.

Enquiry powers

15.32 The Inland Revenue has extensive powers, similar to those in the Taxes Management Act 1970, to enquire into a return or self-certificate. Although most enquiries will be on risk-based selections, some will be randomly selected.[39] A risk is anything that would suggest that a return is incorrect, such as:

---

37 SDLT Manual. para 86230.
38 Sch 11, part 2.
39 SDLT Manual. para 80590.

- errors in the return;

- information suggesting that the purchaser and vendor are connected (eg they share the same address); or

- consideration which places a transaction below an SDLT rate threshold.[40]

15.33 The Inland Revenue can enquire into a return if it gives written notice to the purchaser of its intention to do so before the end of the enquiry period. The enquiry period is nine months after:

1. the filing date if the return was delivered on or before that date;

2. the date on which the return was delivered if the return was delivered after the filing date; or

3. the date on which the return was amended by the purchaser.

15.34 Only one notice of enquiry into a return or amendment can be made.[41]

15.35 Many purchasers and advisers may take comfort from the fact that the Inland Revenue appears to have only a nine-month window of opportunity and can only make one enquiry. It is important to remember, however, that the Inland Revenue also has the power in certain instances to raise a discovery assessment (as discussed in **para 15.45** below) within six years of the effective date or 21 years where there is fraud or negligence.[42]

Scope of enquiry

15.36 An enquiry can extend to anything contained in a return or required to be

---

40 SDLT Manual, para 73040. 42 Sch 10, para 31.
41 Sch 10, para 12.

contained in a return, that relates to whether SDLT is payable or the amount of SDLT payable. In the case of a notice of enquiry that relates to an amendment by the purchaser, the enquiry is confined to the amendment, if the time limit for an enquiry into the return being amended has passed or the return has already been subject to an enquiry.[43]

Notice to produce documents

15.37 An enquiry will begin with a notice in writing requiring the purchaser to produce documents in its possession and power and to provide information as may reasonably be required for the purposes of the enquiry. The notice can be given at the same time as the notice of enquiry and should state the due date for compliance with the request. The purchaser should be given at least 30 days to comply.[44] The Inland Revenue has stated that it will also send to the purchaser a copy of its Code of Practice which explains what the purchaser can expect during the course of an enquiry.[45]

15.38 The purchaser is able to provide copies of documents rather than originals if it chooses. The copies must be photographic or other facsimiles, however, and the Inland Revenue can still require that the originals be produced for inspection.[46]

15.39 The taxpayer can appeal against a notice to produce documents, provided that it is made in writing to the officer of the Board who issued the notice and within 30 days of the issue date of the notice.[47]

---

43 Sch 10, para 13.
44 Sch 10, para 14.
45 SDLT Manual, para 80870.
46 Sch 10, para 14(3).
47 Sch 10, para 15.

Penalties

15.40 A person who fails to comply with a notice to produce documents is liable to a penalty of £50. If the failure continues, they can be liable to a further daily penalty of £30 if the penalty is determined by the Inland Revenue, or £150 if a court determines the failure.[48]

Amending a return during an enquiry

15.41 The Inland Revenue can amend a return by notice in writing if it discovers at the time of the enquiry that there has been an underpayment of SDLT, and an amendment is immediately necessary to prevent a loss of tax.[49] This is known as a jeopardy amendment.[50]

Ending an enquiry

15.42 An enquiry by the Inland Revenue is completed when the Inland Revenue informs the purchaser by way of a closure notice. The closure notice must state that, in the opinion of the Inland Revenue, no amendment is required, or an amendment to a return needs to be made.[51]

15.43 The closure notice takes effect when it is issued. The purchaser can apply to the General or Special Commissioners for a direction that the Inland Revenue must give a closure notice within a specified period. This prevents an open-ended enquiry process being initiated by the Inland Revenue.[52]

---

48 Sch 10, para 16.
49 Sch 10, para 17.
50 SDLT Manual, para 84210.
51 Sch 10, para 23.
52 Sch 10, para 24.

Self-certificates

15.44 The Inland Revenue may also enquire into a self-certificate if it gives notice of its intention to make the enquiry to the purchaser before the end of the enquiry period. The enquiry period is the period nine months after the date on which the self-certificate was produced.[53]

Assessment powers

Discovery assessments

15.45 The Inland Revenue can make an assessment, called a discovery assessment, within six years (extended to 21 years in the case of fraud or negligence) after the effective date of the transaction where it is discovered that:

- an amount of tax that ought to have been assessed has not been assessed;
- an assessment to tax is or has become insufficient; or
- relief has been given that is or has become excessive.[54]

15.46 The discovery assessment will be for the amount which, in the Inland Revenue's opinion, should be charged to make good the loss of tax.

15.47 Where a return has been lodged, the Inland Revenue's power to issue a discovery assessment is restricted to circumstances where:

- there has been fraud or negligence on the part of the purchaser, a partner of the purchaser, or a person acting on behalf of the purchaser; or

---

53 Sch 11, para 7.
54 Sch 10, para 28.

- the time limit to give notice of enquiry has expired or an enquiry has been concluded and, on the basis of the information made available to the Inland Revenue, it could not reasonably have been aware that there was an insufficiency of tax paid.[55]

15.48 Information will be regarded as made available to the Inland Revenue if:

1. it is contained in a land transaction return made by the purchaser;
2. it is contained in any documents produced or information provided to the Inland Revenue for the purposes of an enquiry into any such return; or
3. it is information, the existence of which, could reasonably be expected to be inferred by the Inland Revenue from information falling within **1.** or **2.** above, or has been notified in writing to the Inland Revenue by the purchaser or a person acting on the purchaser's behalf.

15.49 A purchaser should consider, therefore, making full disclosure of a transaction to limit the right of the Inland Revenue to make a discovery assessment.

15.50 The Inland Revenue has no right to make a discovery assessment if the insufficiency of tax is due to a mistake in the return as to the basis on which SDLT ought to have been computed, and the return was made in accordance with practice generally prevailing at the time it was made.[56]

---

55 Sch 10, para 30.
56 Sch 10, para 30(5).

Notice of assessment

15.51 To be valid a notice of discovery assessment must be served on the purchaser and must state the tax due, the date on which the notice is issued, and the time within which any appeal against the assessment can be made.[57]

Relief in the case of excessive assessment

15.52 *Taxed more than once in respect of same matter*: If a person believes it has been assessed more than once in respect of the same transaction, an application can be made in writing for relief. If the Inland Revenue reject the claim, then an appeal can be made to the Commissioners.[58]

15.53 *Mistake in return*: If a person believes that a mistake in a return has led to an overpayment of SDLT, it may make a claim for relief by notice in writing not more than six years after the effective date of the transaction. On receipt of the notice the Inland Revenue will enquire into the matter to determine whether a repayment is due. The taxpayer is precluded from making a claim in respect of a mistake as to the basis on which the liability ought to have been calculated, when the return was in fact made in accordance with practice generally prevailing at the time, or in respect of a mistake in a claim or election included in the return.[59] For example, if a subsequent court decision amends previous prevailing practice, then a purchaser could not claim there had been a mistake.

---

57 Sch 10, para 32.
58 Sch 10, para 33.
59 Sch 10, para 34.

Information powers

15.54 The Inland Revenue has extensive information powers in addition to its enquiry powers. These powers apply not only to purchasers but also to third parties. The Inland Revenue has stated that the powers are intended for important investigations where other information powers are not suitable and should not be used for trivial or unsuitable cases.[60]

15.55 There are three different kinds of information power:

- information powers exercised by an authorised officer of the Inland Revenue;
- information powers exercised by the Board of Inland Revenue; and
- information powers exercisable on an application to a court.

Information powers exercised by an authorised officer of the Inland Revenue

Purchasers and third parties

15.56 An authorised officer of the Inland Revenue can, subject to the limitations discussed in **para 15.61** below, by notice in writing require a purchaser or any third party to deliver such documents as are in that person's possession or power and contain information relevant to any tax liability to which that person is or may be subject to, or to provide such information as may reasonably be required as being relevant to the amount of any liability to tax.[61]

---

60 SDLT Manual, para 80600.
61 Sch 13, parts 1 and 2.

15.57 In order to give a notice, an authorised officer must first obtain the consent of the General or Special Commissioners.[62]

15.58 Where a notice is given to a third party, the taxpayer to whom it relates is entitled to a copy of the notice unless the Commissioners direct otherwise. This would only occur where the taxpayer was accused of fraud.[63]

Tax accountants

15.59 The information powers, subject to the limitations discussed in **para 15.61** below, also allow an authorised officer of the Inland Revenue to demand by notice in writing documents from a tax accountant who is convicted of an offence in relation to tax by a court in the UK, or has a penalty imposed on them for assisting in or inducing the preparation of a return which it knows to be incorrect.[64] Before giving a notice the authorised officer must first get approval from a circuit judge. The tax accountant must be given at least 30 days to comply with the notice.[65]

15.60 To comply with a notice a taxpayer, third party or tax accountant (as the case may be) may provide copies instead of originals.[66]

Restrictions on information powers

15.61 The information powers exercisable by an authorised officer of the Inland Revenue are subject to certain restrictions.[67] These are:

---

62 Sch 13, para 2.
63 Sch 13, para 9.
64 Sch 13, para 14.

65 Sch 13, paras 16 and 17.
66 Sch 13, para 23.
67 Sch 13, para 19.

1. Certain personal records (eg items relating to a person's physical or mental health) or journalistic material cannot be required.[68] (Journalistic material means material acquired or created for the purposes of journalism.)

2. The Inland Revenue cannot require a person to deliver documents or provide information relating to the conduct of any appeal relating to tax.[69]

3. A notice may not be given to a barrister, advocate or solicitor by an authorised officer of the Board, but only by the Board itself.[70]

4. A person is not obliged to deliver or make available a document the whole of which originates more than six years before the date of the notice. That said, the Inland Revenue may issue a notice which excludes the six-year restriction if the General or Special Commissioners give consent to that notice having the exclusion.[71]

5. An auditor is not in general required to produce any documents that are their property which were created in connection with the performance of their statutory functions.

6. A tax adviser is not in general required to produce documents that are their property consisting of communications between them and a client where the purpose of the communications was to provide tax advice.[72]

7. The power of the Inland Revenue to require documents from a third party or a tax accountant does not oblige a barrister, advocate or solicitor to deliver or make available, without client consent, any document with respect to which a claim to legal professional privilege could be maintained.[73]

---

68 Sch 13, para 20. Personal and journalistic records are defined in ss 12 and 13 of the Police and Criminal Evidence Act 1984.
69 Sch 13, para 21.
70 Sch 13, para 22.
71 Sch 13, para 24.
72 Sch 13, para 26.
73 Sch 13, para 25.
74 Sch 13, para 35.

15.62 In this case, items subject to legal privilege has been defined to mean:[74]

1. communications between a professional legal adviser and their client or any person representing their client made in connection with the giving of legal advice to the client;

2. communications between a professional legal adviser and their client or any person representing their client, or between an adviser or their client or any such representative and any other person, made in connection with or in contemplation of legal proceedings and for the purposes of such proceedings; and

3. items enclosed with or referred to in such communications and made:

   - in connection with the giving of legal advice, or
   - in connection with or in contemplation of legal proceedings and for the purposes of such proceedings,

   when they are in the possession of a person entitled to possess them.

15.63 Note that items held with the intention of furthering a criminal purpose are not subject to privilege.

15.64 The SDLT code provides that where there is a dispute over legal professional privilege, such disputes should be referred to a court for resolution.[75]

15.65 Although the SDLT code seeks to define the extent of legal professional privilege, it is important to bear in mind that this privilege is recognised as a fundamental human right established in common law, and is

---

75 SI 2837/2003, para 38.   **76** [2002] STC 786.

part of the right of privacy guaranteed in Article 8 of the Convention for the Protection of Human Rights and Fundamental Freedoms. The case of *R (Morgan Grenfell & Co Ltd) v Special Commissioner of Taxation*[76] makes it clear that this right can only be overridden by express statement or necessary implication.

Information powers exercisable by the Board

15.66 The Board may require a person to deliver documents in its possession or power where the Board has reasonable grounds for believing that a person has failed to comply with any provision of the SDLT code, or that a failure may seriously prejudice the proper assessment or collection of tax. The only stated exception to this power is in respect of personal records or journalistic material.[77]

Information powers exercisable on application to a court

15.67 A court can require a person to deliver documents if satisfied, on information on oath given by an authorised officer, that there are reasonable grounds for suspecting that an offence involving serious fraud in connection with, or in relation to, SDLT has been or is about to be committed and that the documents are necessary for the purposes of any proceedings in respect of such an offence. The order can require documents to be delivered within ten working days or any shorter period as the order may specify. Documents subject to legal professional privilege are excluded from an order.[78]

---

77 Sch 13, paras 28-31.
78 Sch 13, paras 32-35.

Entry with warrant to obtain evidence of offence

15.68 A court may, if satisfied on information on oath given by an officer of the Board, that there are reasonable grounds for suspecting that an offence involving serious fraud in connection with SDLT is being or is about to be committed, and that evidence of it is to be found on premises specified in the information, issue a warrant authorising an officer of the Board to enter premises if necessary.[79]

15.69 An offence involves serious fraud if its commission has led, or is intended or likely to lead, to substantial financial gain to any person, or to serious prejudice to the proper assessment or collection of tax.[80]

15.70 Note that the power to enter with a warrant to obtain information does not apply to premises occupied for the purposes of the Crown.[81] If a raid is in progress, an adviser should send suitably qualified persons to provide legal and moral support and to ensure the terms of the warrant are being complied with.

Power to inspect premises

15.71 The Board of Inland Revenue can authorise an officer of the Inland Revenue to inspect any property for the purposes of ascertaining its market value or any other matter connected with SDLT. A person who delays or obstructs an officer commits an offence and is liable to a fine.[82]

---

79 Sch 13, para 43.
80 Sch 13, para 44.
81 S 107(3).
82 S 94.

Collection powers

15.72 Where tax is due and payable the Inland Revenue may make a demand for the sum charged from the person liable to pay it. If a person neglects or refuses to pay the sum charged upon demand, the Inland Revenue may distrain upon the goods and chattels of the person charged.[83]

Rulings

15.73 Although the adjudication process commonly associated with group, reconstruction on acquisition relief under stamp duty no longer exists, under SDLT the Inland Revenue will give pre- and post-transaction rulings in accordance with Code of Practice 10.[84] Applicants should review the Code, which details the information required by the Inland Revenue before a ruling will be given. The ruling request should be sent to the purchaser's local Stamp Office.

15.74 The existence of a ruling procedure means that there is now scope for a purchaser to satisfy itself of the SDLT treatment of a transaction prior to entering into it.

---

83 Sch 12, paras 2-3.
84 SDLT Manual, para 51000.

Appendix – completing SDLT returns

SDLT1

- The Inland Revenue's instructions for completing SDLT return forms 1-4 can be found in Inland Revenue publication SDLT6, Land Transaction Return Guidance Notes.
- Use an original form (because they are bar-coded) – photocopies are not acceptable except where an amended return is to be submitted.
- Write in black ink (including the purchaser's signature) and capitals.
- If you make a mistake, do not use whitener, but cross out and write the correction to the right or below the box.
- Do not cross out boxes or mark them 'not applicable' – leave them blank.
- The form must be signed by the purchaser. Agents (such as solicitors) cannot sign it, unless they hold a power of attorney. A person signing under a power of attorney should write 'Power of Attorney' after their signature.
- When entering sums of money, do not use commas (ie £50000 not £50,000).

Where the land transaction is the completion of a contract which has already been substantially performed, the second land transaction due on completion is not sent to the Netherton Processing Centre, but to the Manchester Stamp Office (see **para 14.55**):

Manchester Stamp Office
Upper Fifth Floor
Royal Exchange
Exchange Street
Manchester M2 7EB
DX: 1430 Manchester 2
Tel: 0161 834 8020

The Manchester Stamp Office will intervene in the process at Netherton in relation to the first land transaction return submitted on substantial performance to ensure that SDLT is charged only once.

The land transaction return on completion will be identical to the return submitted on substantial performance (unless further unexpected consideration is payable on completion), except that Box 15 will state that no amount is enclosed with the notification.

Box 1 – the property is residential (01), mixed (02) or non-residential (03) (ie commercial).

Box 2 – the transaction is a conveyance/transfer (including an assignment of a lease and a surrender for consideration) and the substantial performance of a contract of sale (F), the grant of a lease (including the substantial performance of an agreement for lease) (L) or something else (O).

Box 3 – freehold with vacant possession (FP), freehold subject to long lease at ground rent (FG), freehold subject to occupational leases (FT), long lease at ground rent with vacant possession (LG), long lease subject to occupational lease (LT), occupational leases (grant or assignment) (LP), and others (OT – which includes a reversionary lease).

Box 4 – the effective date of the transaction (see **paras 2.15-2.30**). This is a crucial piece of information – failure to provide this is a common reason for rejection of a return.

Box 5 – mention any unusual restrictions or covenants. Generally the expression 'ordinary covenants and conditions' should suffice. The question covers similar ground to the PD form under stamp duty. The Guidance Notes give examples of the type of covenants that would need to be specifically mentioned, including a right to buy the property back at less than market value, user covenants restricting the use of a shop to a particular trade, and an 'agricultural occupancy condition'.

Box 7 – only fill this in where the transaction is an exchange of properties. We understand that this would not apply to a surrender and regrant of a lease.

Box 9 – claim relief, for example disadvantaged areas (various codes for commercial, residential and mixed), group relief (12) or charity relief (20). There is a code for miscellaneous reliefs (28) which would be used, for example, for sale and leaseback transactions, the PFI relief and part-exchanges with property traders.

Additional information is requested if the purchaser is a charity (Registered Charity number) or a house-building company (Construction Industry Scheme reference).

Box 10 – if no consideration is given, then generally no return needs to be completed. However, if the land transaction is the completion of a contract which has been substantially performed, a land transaction return needs to be completed stating the full consideration, but which should be sent to the Manchester Stamp Office (see above). If consideration of £1 is given for a transfer, then a return must be lodged but no SDLT would be payable. Note that if the option to waive the exemption from VAT has been exercised, then SDLT would be payable on the purchase price plus VAT unless (in the case of rented property) the transfer is of a going concern.

Box 11 – show any VAT separately.

Box 14 – Round down the figure to the nearest pound. If no tax is due (for example, if the price is below £150,000 for non-residential property) put £0.00 in the box – do not leave it blank or write 'nil'.

Box 15 – The payment amount enclosed with the return may be different from Box 14 if it includes interest and/or penalties, if moneys have already been paid on account of SDLT, if the transaction has already been substantially performed or if an application has been made to defer payment in the case of contingent or unascertained consideration.

Boxes 16-25 – Fill in Boxes 16-22 when either:

- the transaction is the grant of a new lease; or
- you are buying a property subject to leases (unless authorised by the Inland Revenue to do otherwise).

In the first case, complete also Boxes 23-25.

Box 17 – refer to **para 5.70** regarding the term of a lease for SDLT purposes, which does not necessarily correspond to the stated contractual term.

Box 20 – only include VAT if the landlord has actually elected. Only in the case of stepped rents can the increase (only include those in the first five years of lease unless they are abnormal) be included in the calculation.

Box 23 – put the NPV of the rents here.

Where the transaction is the grant of a new commercial lease, complete SDLT4, but no SDLT 4 need be completed in relation to leases where the transaction reported is a sale to which the leases are subject.

Where the transaction is the purchase of a property subject to several leases, give the details for each lease. There is only room for one on the form, so put the rest on a separate sheet of paper. If buying, for example, a shopping centre with many leases, ring the SDLT enquiry line to agree an approach.

Box 26 – each title number or unregistered title is treated as a separate property. Where more than one piece of land is sold, this needs to be made clear here and an SDLT3 also needs to be completed. In the case of a block transfer of many properties, the Guidance Notes indicate that it will not be necessary to complete a separate SDLT3 for each.

Box 27 – when a return is lodged and SDLT paid, a certificate will be issued to the purchaser by the Inland Revenue. The certificate (SDLT5) must be produced to the Land Registry if the purchaser wishes to register its interest. In general, a single cer-tificate is issued for one return. However, a purchaser can, if more than one interest is reported in a single return, request that a separate certificate is issued for each.

Box 29 – see the appendix to the Guidance Notes for the local authority code number.

Box 31 – the SDLT1 can still be lodged if no property identification number from the National Land and Property Gazetteer can be found.

Box 33 – if attaching a plan, put the form reference number on it together with the address or description of the land given on the form and the local authority code. The plan does not need to be to scale, but it does need to say so if that is the case. Any scale should be shown on it.

Boxes 34-39 and 45-48 – if there are more than two vendors/landlords/grantors put the additional ones on form SDLT2. A company vendor's address is its registered office. There is no requirement to name multiple vendors in a particular order. If the name of the vendor is more than 28 characters long, the name may either be abbreviated or only the first 28 letters of the name provided.

Boxes 39-44 – 'agent' includes a solicitor or conveyancer.

Boxes 49-59 – if there are more than two purchasers/tenants/grantees, put the additional details on form SDLT2. If the name of the purchaser is more than 28 characters long, the name may either be abbreviated or only the first 28 letters of the name provided. Again, a company purchaser's address is its registered office. The purchasers are jointly and severally liable for the SDLT and thus again the order of their names is not important. If the name does not fit, this must be brought to the attention of the Inland Revenue in some way to ensure the form of certificate will state the full name of the purchaser. Note in Box 56 to give the purchaser's contact number. Advisers should tick Box 58 for the certificate to come back to the agent and Box 59 to authorise the Stamp Office to send copies of correspondence to the agent.

Boxes 60-64 – 'agent' includes a solicitor or conveyancer.

Box 71 – the declaration must be signed by the purchaser, not the agent, unless the agent holds a power of attorney in which case they should put the words 'Power of

Attorney' under the signature. In the case of a company, the signature must be that of a proper officer who can act on the company's behalf, such as the company secretary or a director. It is recommended that the same parties who are executing the transaction document sign the return. The signature should be in black ink.

SDLT2

Use this form where there are more than two vendors or purchasers. Add the reference number from the payslip on form SDLT1. The purchasers named on the form must sign it.

SDLT3

Use this form where all the property details will not fit on form SDLT1. Again, add the reference number from the payslip on form SDLT1. On a large portfolio purchase, contact the SDLT enquiry line on 0845 603 0135, who may be able to help avoid filling in multiple forms.

SDLT4

Use this form where:

- the transaction is the grant of a lease, a business sale agreement, the purchaser is a company, SDLT is to be paid in instalments or mineral rights are reserved; or
- any payments are contingent or uncertain.

Again, add the reference number from the payslip on form SDLT1.

Box 9 – Specify if a former lease was surrendered. There appear to be no situations where a term of a lease could be surrendered without the lease being surrendered. This could include some variations that take effect on a surrender and regrant (ie where the term and/or demise are altered).

Box 12 – Contingent reserved rent (eg conditional on planning permission). Examples of unascertained rent which is not turnover rent are geared rent or rent-sharing leases (see **Chapter 5**).